D0407593

THE NOBLE HUSTLE

ALSO BY COLSON WHITEHEAD

Zone One
Sag Harbor
Apex Hides the Hurt
The Colossus of New York
John Henry Days
The Intuitionist

DOUBLEDAY

New York   London   Toronto   Sydney   Auckland

THE
NOBLE HUSTLE

POKER, BEEF JERKY AND DEATH

Colson Whitehead

All rights reserved. Published in the United States by Doubleday, a division of Random House LLC, New York, and in Canada by Random House of Canada Limited, Toronto, Penguin Random House companies.

www.doubleday.com

DOUBLEDAY and the portrayal of an anchor with a dolphin are registered trademarks of Random House LLC.

Portions of this book were previously published, in different form, as "Occasional Dispatches from the Republic of Anhedonia" in *Grantland* (July 2011).

Book design by Maria Carella
Jacket design and illustration by Rodrigo Corral Design

Library of Congress Cataloging-in-Publication Data
Whitehead, Colson, 1969–
    The noble hustle : poker, beef jerky and death / Colson Whitehead.
        pages cm
    1. World Series of Poker. 2. Poker. 3. Gambling. 4. Whitehead,
Colson, 1969– I. Title.
    GV1254.W45 2014
    795.412—dc23   2013031448

ISBN 978-0-385-53705-6
ISBN 978-0-385-53706-3 (eBook)

MANUFACTURED IN THE UNITED STATES OF AMERICA

10 9 8 7 6 5 4 3 2 1

First Edition

FOR ALISON RICH
who made people pick up a book about elevator inspectors

an-he-do-nia: the inability to experience pleasure

CONTENTS

THE NOBLE HUSTLE

THE
REPUBLIC
OF ANHEDONIA

I have a good poker face because I am half dead inside. My particular combo of slack features, negligible affect, and soulless gaze has helped my game ever since I started playing twenty years ago, when I was ignorant of pot odds and M-theory and four-betting, and it gave me a boost as I collected my trove of lore, game by game, hand by hand. It has not helped me human relationships—wise over the years, but surely I'm not alone here. Anyone whose peculiar mix of genetic material and formative experiences has resulted in a near-expressionless mask can relate. Nature giveth, taketh, etc. You make the best of the hand you're dealt.

This thing draped over my skull and fastened by muscle is also a not-too-bad public-transportation face, a kind of wretched camouflage, which would come in handy on my trip to Atlantic City. Flash this mug and people don't mess with you on buses, and this day I was heading to training camp. I had six weeks to get in shape. I was being staked to play in the World Series of Poker for a magazine, and my regular game was a five-dollar buy-in where catching up with friends took precedence over pulverizing your opponents.

There was no question about taking a bus. I'm of that subset of native New Yorkers who can't drive. Every spring, I made noises about getting my license and checked out the websites of local driving schools, which as a species embodied the most retrograde web design on the internet, real Galápagos stuff, replete with frenetic logos and fonts they don't make anymore, the HTML flourishes of the previous century. How could I give my money to a business with so incompetent a portal? My wife and I owned a car, and she drove us everywhere, which came to be a hassle. I used to joke that I was afraid of getting my license—that I was at a point in my life that the first time I got behind the wheel, I'd just keep driving. The first couple of times I made this joke, people laughed. Then maybe my delivery began to falter, there was a change in tone, and they'd look around nervously, peek over my shoulder for another person to talk to. My wife had the car now. We got divorced four days prior.

I'd been looking forward to a descent into some primo degradation to start my trip, a little atmosphere to match my mood, but of course the Port Authority was cleaned up now, like the rest of the city. In the daytime, anyway. Across the street, the shining *New York Times* tower watched over the entryway, a beacon of truth and justice and Renzo Piano, and inside the terminal corridors the stores were scrubbed nightly, well-buffed, the reassuring and familiar places you've shopped at plenty. Duane Reade, Hudson News, the kiosks of big banks yet to fail. I could be anywhere, starting a journey to anyplace, a new life or a funeral.

I rushed to make the 3:30 bus and thought I'd have to gulp down a hot dog from a street vendor—fearing a grim return of said frank hours later at the table—but had time to pick up an albacore tuna sandwich with dill, capers, and lemon mayo on marbled rye, plus an artisanal root cola, all for ten bucks across the street at Dean and DeLuca. Estimated Probability of Degradation: down 35 percent.

I waited to board and saw I didn't need a public-transportation face. The other passengers queued up for AC were exfoliated and fit, heading down for Memorial Day fun, not the disreputable lot of Port Authority legend. Their weekend bags gave no indication that they contained their owners' sole possessions. Where have all the molesters gone, the weenie wagglers and chicken hawks? Whither the diddlers? The only shabby element I registered was the signage at the Greyhound and Peter Pan counters, still showcasing the dependable logos remembered from the bad trips of yore. Returning from a botched assignation or misguided attempt to reconnect with an old friend. Rumbling and put-putting to a scary relative's house in bleak winter as you peered out into the gray mush through green, trapezoid windows. Greyhounds were raised in deplorable puppy mills and drugged up for the racetrack, I think I read somewhere, and Peter Pan used to enter kids' bedrooms and entice them, so perhaps there is a core aspect to the bus industry that defies rebranding.

The bus was state of the art, like it had wi-fi, and even though I sat two rows up from the lav I did not smell it. It was two and a half hours to AC, plenty of time for me to graze on my inadequacies. Poker eminence Doyle Brunson called Hold'em "the Cadillac of poker," and I was only qualified to steer a Segway. In one of the fiction-writing manuals, it says that there are only two stories: a hero goes on a journey, and a stranger comes to town. I don't know. This being life, and not literature, we'll have to make do with this: A middle-aged man, already bowing and half broken under his psychic burdens, decides to take on the stress of being one of the most unqualified players in the history of the Big Game. A hapless loser goes on a journey, a strange man comes to gamble.

According to the two crew cuts in the row in front of me, the weekly pool party at their casino was killer, but I wasn't going to make it over there. I hit my poker book, cramming. "Big raises make big pots." "Before you enter a pot, think about who the likely flop bettor will be." The highway bored through miles of Jersey's old growth, as if the forests had been mowed down specifically for passage to our destination, a tunnel to the Land of Atrocious Odds, and then we broke off the expressway and the big gambling houses burst up, looming over the gray water. We passed the one- and two-story buildings of downtown Atlantic City—clapboard homes, broken chapels, purveyors of quick cash—that seemed washed up against the casinos like driftwood and soda bottles. Then we pulled into the Leisure Industrial Complex.

Growing up in the city, I never went to a lot of malls, so I didn't have the psychological scars of my Midwestern friends, who cringed at the thought of all the adolescent afternoons spent mindlessly drifting across the buffed tile. I like the Leisure Industrial Complex when I can find it, those meticulously arranged consumer arenas. I don't care if it's a suburban galleria sucking the human plankton into itself from the exit ramps or a metro-area monolith stuffed with escalators to convey the herd to the multiple price-pointed retail outlets, food court stalls, and movie screens.

Gimme a red-brick pedestrian mall reclaimed from urban blight and dolled up to commemorate some location of inflated historical import—I love those guys. There is the multiplicity of diversion, sure, but more important is that a sector of human endeavor is diligently trying to improve itself and succeeding spectacularly. Consumer theorists, commercial architects, scientists of demography are working hard to make the LIC better, more efficient, more perfect. They analyze the traffic patterns and microscopic eye movements of shoppers, the implications of rest room and water fountain placement, and disseminate their innovations for the universal good. Even if we fail ourselves in a thousand ways every day, we can depend on this one grace in our lives. We are in good hands.

Anyone who's gambled in the past twenty years knows that casinos are high rollers in the LIC. The contemporary casino is more than a gambling destination; it's a multifarious pleasure enclosure intended to satisfy every member of the family unit. Reimagined as resorts, there's moderate-stakes blackjack for Dad, a sea-salt spa scrub for Mom, the cortex-agitating arcade for the youngsters—or the Men's Mani-Pedi Suite for Dad, Pai Gau Poker for Mom, and Highly Supervised Kidz Camp for the little ones (once you sign the liability waiver).

A mall with living rooms. The concept of such a thing, to eat, drink, and play, and then dream inside its walls. No windows, for what sight could be more inspiring than your true self laid bare, with all its hungers and flaws and grubby aspirations. Stroll past the high-end shops with accented names, recognizable theme restaurants owned by TV chefs, indoor Big Tops, man-made wave pools, and find nourishment for any desire zipping through your brain. If there's a gap in perimeter through which an unfulfilled wish might escape, it will be plugged by your next trip.

They even have bus depots. Some casinos are equipped with snap-on bus depots, an optional component for the base model. Like the Tropicana. Today's outpost of the LIC was the Tropicana, local franchise of the famous Vegas standby, where James Bond busted heads in *Diamonds Are Forever*. Methinks he did not arrive on Greyhound. You might escape if the bus didn't pull directly into the building itself, so the depot was a worthy investment. Some of the passengers stood and funneled to the door, causing a scandal. "Where is he going?" "They're not waiting for their bonus?" Meaning the twenty-dollar voucher they give you to play upstairs—it's worked out between Greyhound and the casino (they really want you to stay). For what kind of inhuman monster didn't wait for their bonus—it's free money.

I jumped up and joined the apostates. I was vibrating with newly acquired poker knowledge and couldn't wait. The smell of ancient cigarette smoke and the mellow undertones of men's room disinfectant were an intoxicant. I checked in, chucked in some buffalo wings for fuel, and soon I was in the Tropicana Poker Room.

I found my degradation. You can rubble the old Times Square and erect magnificent corporate towers, hose down Port Authority and clean under its fingernails, but you can't change people. I was among gamblers.

I sat down at a $1/$2 table with types I would encounter with some frequency during my training. Like Big Mitch. Big Mitch is a potbellied endomorph in fabric-softened khaki shorts and polo shirt, a middle-aged white guy here with his wife, who was off dropping chips on the roulette felt according to her patented system. Fully equipped with a mortgage, a decent job, and disposable income. The segments of his thick metal watchband chick-chicked on his hairy wrist each time he entered the pot. Your average home player. What Big Mitch wants the most, apart from coming home to see that young Kaitlyn hasn't had a party and wrecked the house while they were away (she's really been acting out lately, but Pat says all girls go through that stage), is to brag to his home-game buddies and certain guys at the office of how much he won tonight, with a breakdown of a Really Big Hand or two. He will be less vocal about his failures, as we all are.

Next to two Big Mitches was a Methy Mike, a harrowed man who had been tested in untold skirmishes, of which the poker table was only one. If Methy Mike had been hitched, the lady had packed her bags long ago, and if they had spawned, their parenting goals probably ended with making sure their kid didn't get a tattoo on her face, and they did not always succeed. Often locals,

Methy Mikes are on a first-name basis with the bosses and dealers and cocktail waitresses, and you can count on hearing a little catching up. "Haven't seen you in a while." "I've been . . . had some stuff come up." So I see. Iggy Pop takes a look at these guys and says, "Wow, he's really let himself go."

They are weathered by the sun, by their lifestyles, which you can only guess at, the underlying narrative of their decay, and resemble unfortunates who have been dragged on chains from the back of a beat-up van and left to desiccate in the desert, like one of the down-and-outers in *The Treasure of the Sierra Madre*. Undone by their hardwired inclinations and undying dream of a new start. "Can you help a fellow American who's down on his luck?" Luck—they believe in luck, its patterns, its unknowable rules. They will, seeing pocket Jacks demolish some weekend punter, tell the table, "Let me tell you a sad story about a pair a Jacks." A sad story for every hand, every one of the 1,326 possible starting combinations.

And then there was Robotron, wedged in there, lean and wiry and hunkered down, a young man with sunglasses and earbuds, his hoodie cinched tight around his face like a school shooter or a bathroom loiterer. Weaned on internet play, Robotron is only here tonight because the Feds shut down all the U.S. online poker sites a month ago. Black Friday, something about money laundering. Here with the humans. Otherwise the Robotrons would be back in their childhood rooms, eight pixelated tables open on the screen; he can play eight games at once, zip zip. It's not so hard once you retrain those pathways in the brain, cramming decades of poker experience into eighteen months. Why leave the house at all, between the poker sites and the porn sites? What are other people for, but for robbing or fucking? (The goddamned Feds, breeding a new generation of libertarians in the subdivs.) Real people, talking, breathing, it must be so weird to them. Their earbuds help keep 'em out, playing music, self-help manuals, *If I'm So Wonderful, Why Am I Still Single?* as read by Edward James Olmos, or the latest invasion plans transmitted from their home planet.

There was one woman at the table, a quiet sixty-something lady with bright red hair, the follicles of which it was perhaps possible to count. Five percent of commercially available hair dyes actually match a color that occurs in nature. Hers was not one of them. I liked her.

I will now take a moment to explain Hold'em to the lay reader, I don't mind. In my home games, I often assumed the mantle of the Explainer, laying out the rules for the newbies—the indulging girlfriend, the language poet in town for the weekend, and, maddeningly, people I had played with dozens of times before. I wrote the hand rankings on a little piece of paper for them to keep by their chips, reminded them it's "one or two or none from your hand, and three or four or five from the board." I stopped being so amenable once my kid started talking because I was explaining shit all the time now. "Daddy, why is the sky blue?" "Daddy, how do fish swim?" "Daddy, where shall I keep my secret fears of the world, and tend to them like my private garden?" Nowadays my poker neophytes are on their own.

You start with two cards. You know what an ante is, my friend, even if you have never played a single hand of poker. Gotta pay to play, that's the American way, sweet pea, whether it's parking meters or X-ray specs. In Hold'em, only two people plop down an automatic bet without seeing their cards: the Small Blind and the Big Blind. Blind, because you're in a dark mine probably about to step into the abyss. Depending on the stakes, the Small Blind is one dollar and the Big Blind is two dollars (or twenty-five cents and fifty cents, thirty dollars and sixty dollars, whatever). This way there are always two people invested in the hand, to different degrees. They're in, and maybe they're protective of their opening contribution, will feel moved to defend their one dollar or two dollars, the way a parent on a playground might steer their progeny away from that weird kid who's been eating nuggets from the sandbox (feral cats use this place as their bathroom at night, according to a parenting blog).

If the rest of the players at the table, a maximum of ten, want to enter the hand, they have to match (or call) the Big Blind of two dollars or fifty cents or whatever, or raise it, or fold. And so on for the others ringed around the table, until it comes back to the Small Blind, who has to bring up his initial forced bet to match whatever the current bet is. Finally, the Big Blind, who, also having bet without seeing her cards, can match or raise, because they want to protect their little tyke, or because they got a monster hand, you never know. Two dollars is two dollars, we live in a capitalist society.

Everything begins and ends with these two cards. You are the ant: They squeeze you like the fingers of a mean kid. You have to learn which combos are worth engaging and which are not. For example: For three years I was cursed with sitting down in the exact wrong seat at group dinners. Wholly and inescapably hexed. Adjacent to a blowhard lush, between two narcissistic twerps, face-to-face with the mime. You look at what you've been dealt and think, *This will end badly*, and check out of the convo and endure until next time. Or maybe you make the best of a bad situation and play the affability game, go for it, but your optimism is only rarely rewarded. The lush starts talking about "immigrants," the narcissists discuss that new boutique colonic joint, the mime won't shut up. Once in a while, though, you have a pretty swell time with that unpromising start, and it is these improbable nights that feed the gambling delusion. "If it worked once, I can make it happen again." (The dinner analogy makes the most sense to misanthropes, I reckon.)

Then comes the Flop: three communal cards in the middle of the table. Sharing with strangers—we've moved from capitalism to communism. Flop, like you've parachuted into the war zone and landed in a strategic position, or the champs at air command have miscalculated again and dropped you smack in the enemy trenches. Everyone checks, bets, raises, or folds according to their present coordinates. Checking is ducking from artillery, like if I lie low maybe I won't get hit and my lot will improve. Taking a second to see what's going on.

Then comes the next communal card, the Turn, as in: Turn the corner to see the next obstacle fate has thrown in your path, three goddamned tourists walking shoulder to shoulder so you can't progress, or a block party hosted by Everyone You Owe E-mail To. You have improved, or not. Finally we get to the last card, the River, and fortune's drifts and eddies have borne you to a safe harbor, or you suddenly discover that pirates crept aboard a few rounds ago and you're about to be robbed: Hold'em.

About Limit and No Limit: I have good card sense, I'm a pretty good player in my five-dollar buy-in game, in the way that a lot of people are good in low-stakes games. The size of the bets is capped, "limited," so people hang around to the River waiting for a miracle, and why not, you can always buy in for another few bucks. Let's say when you're playing cheap at Mike's on Saturday night, the maximum bet might be one buck—there will be no handing over the keys to the Prius. On a bad night you lose forty dollars, cheaper than the date nights you regularly schedule in the hope of "keeping things fresh," cheaper than tromping off to one of the crappy 3-D movies, what with the price of popcorn going through the roof. Over five hours, you got your money's worth. At the $1/$2 chump game I was playing at the Trop, the Small Blind was one dollar and the Big Blind was two dollars.

In No Limit, that's where you get the ladies and gentlemen dropping their genitals on the table, declaring "All in!" You can bet your whole stash, it's crazy. Exciting! Thrill of Gambling! That's what they were playing one table over from me. Fewer Methy Mikes there, and no ladies, crimson hair or no. No Limit is what the boys play these days. The stakes are intensified, but if you bust out, you can still buy back in. In a home game, you can sometimes reach into your pocket and throw a dollar in, if the hand has gotten interesting and you want to keep playing. In a casino, you can only throw in the chips you already have in front of you. That's the cap on your All In. But if you bust out, you can pad over to the ATM machine, pay a strip-club-worthy service charge, and get a new stack of chips.

In a tournament, if you go All In and lose, you're out.

Tonight was a warm-up. Tomorrow I was playing

in my first casino tournament. Ever since I'd taken this assignment, I'd been playing poorly, trying to apply the half-digested poker knowledge I'd gulleted down from books, crashing and burning. If I couldn't maintain a decent level of play in a home game, how could I face the Big Boys in Vegas?

I hadn't slept in weeks. I had to make something happen tonight, even at this crappy $1/$2 table, just for morale's sake. The $1/$2 limit is the crummiest card game available in the modern casino. If it were street retail, it'd be a combo KFC–Taco Bell–Donate Blood Here. You can make a little money playing top hands, but you'll rarely bluff everyone out because staying in until the Magical River is not expensive. In Vegas, I'd be playing with people who didn't bother with these crap stakes.

Next to me, Big Mitch shuffled the top two chips of his disappearing stack. The money could have been so many things. A new propane tank for the grill, or an anniversary dinner with Pat at that new fusion place. Methy Mike ordered another Jack and Coke and tipped the waitress with a dollar chip and a "Thanks, darling." Robotron could see right through our meat and straight into our poker souls, groaning as he announced, "I have to fold to your Ace-Queen." (The goddamned Feds!) The Lady with the Crimson Hair fondled her chips, and I

♦

played tight and won eighty-one dollars. Chicken feed, but enough to cover the entrance fee for tomorrow's tournament.

I toasted my success in A Dam Good Sports Bar upstairs in The Quarter, the casino's dining concourse, meant to evoke Havana. The home of the original Trop, back in the day. It would do. The table next to me ordered 40s of Bud Light, which arrived on ice in buckets. Is that how they celebrated in Cuba's gambling heyday? They toasted the night's festivities, just a few sips away.

I had been here before, in American cities of a certain size, a bunch of gnawed wing bones before me. Drinking beer alone among flat-screens and dead eyes. What happens in Vegas stays in Vegas, because in the end, whatever goes down, whatever you get up to, your triumphs and transgressions, nobody actually understands what it means except for you. What did it mean to you in your secret heart to win that money or lose that money, to hold that person. To see them walk away. It is unshareable. No one to narc on you to the folks back home: The only narc here is you.

Because I was in AC, Vegas's little cousin, the stakes— the highs and lows—were smaller scale. I wanted to tell someone, I won eighty-one bucks. But who cared about eighty-one bucks? Who'd care that I had just started a journey that would take me from my crappy New York apartment, a.k.a. the Our Lady of Perpetual Groaning, and out into the American desert, where I'd be bullied, bluffed, and tested by the best poker players in the world. As it often did when I thought about chicken wings and entropy, my mind turned to Emerson. "Life is a journey, not a destination." Now that was one stone-cold mother-fucker who was not afraid to deliver the truth: After the torments of the journey, you have been well-prepared for the agonies of the destination.

The table next to me ordered another bucket of 40s. They had their expedition, and I had mine.

I returned to my room. I was going to hit the books again before the 11:00 a.m. starting time. My bed was impossibly stiff, as if all the years of bad luck in this place, the busted hopes and evaporated rent money, had been turned into cement, cut into slabs, and then wheeled down the carpeted hallways into the rooms. We slept atop our sarcophagi. I realized I hadn't told anyone where I was going, some real hobo shit. My ex-wife and the kid were upstate, engaged in holiday-weekend good-ness. Here I was acting as if I had nobody. One of the overlooked benefits of joint custody is that you're going to go max thirty-six hours until someone discovers your decomposing body. "Anyone seen him? He was supposed to pick her up after school."

I had people. I flashed to how happy my daughter

was when I told her I won a hundred bucks in a game last summer. I'd driven down to AC with two pals, on the Manboob Express, and brought back one uncashed dollar chip to give her as a souvenir. "One hundred dollars!" Here's a tip for new parents: Start lowering those expectations early, it's going to pay off later. She believed in me. I was her dad.

I was lucky.

I was gonna play in the Big Game and give it my best shot. It was not the National Series of Poker, it was the World Series of Poker, and I would represent my country, the Republic of Anhedonia. We have no borders, but the population teems. No one has deigned to write down our history, but we are an ancient land, founded during the original disappointments, when the first person met another person. I would do it for my countrymen, the shut-ins, the doom-struck, the morbid of temperament, for all those who walk through life with poker faces 24/7 because they never learned any other way. For the gamblers of every socioeconomic station, working class, middle class, upper class, broke-ass; for the sundry gamers twelve stories below, tossing chips into the darkness; for the internet wraiths maniacally clicking before their LCDs in ill-lit warrens in Akron, Boise, and Bhopal, who should really get out more; for all the amateurs who need this game as a sacred haven once a month, who seek the sanctuary of Draw and Stud, where there are never any wild cards and you can count on a good hand every once in a while. For Big Mitch and Methy Mike, Robotron and the Lady with the Crimson Hair, the ones who would kill to go to Vegas and will never make it there, my people all of them. Did I sound disdainful of them before? It was recognition you heard. I contain multitudes, most of them flawed.

Plus, I've always wanted to wear sunglasses indoors.

♦

MAKING
THE NATURE SCENE

In the spring of 2011, I received an e-mail from the editor of a new magazine. He asked if I wanted to write something about sports.

No, I said. I didn't follow sports. Sure, now and then I mixed it up in a Who Had the Most Withholding Father contest with chums, but that's as far as it went for me competitive sports–wise. More important, I was catching my breath after pulling out of a long skid. I had recently finished writing a novel about a city overrun by the living dead, and the plunge into autobiography had left me depleted. I'd barely gone out in months, devoting myself to meeting a moronic deadline I'd imposed in a spasm of optimism. Dating was a distraction, even the frequent-buyer card at my local coffee place was too much of a commitment. Now that I was done with the book, I was starting to feel human again. I wanted to rejoin society, do whatever it is that normal people do when they get together. Drink hormone-free, humanely slaughtered beer. Eat micro-chickens. Compare sadnesses, things of that sort.

The editor had heard that I liked poker—what if they sent me to cover the World Series of Poker?

No, I said. I did indeed like poker, and although there was no way he could know it, was very fond of Las Vegas. But ten days in the desert, in the middle of July? I chap easily. And again, I wanted to give myself a break. In the past year I had devoted myself to the novel and to figuring out the rules of solo parenthood. If I wasn't writing, I was hitting the "Activities for Kids" sites in search of stuff for the kid and I to do on the weekends. It was a hard job, tracing a safe route through the minefield of face-painting, peanut-free caroling, and assorted pony bullshit that would get us safely to dinnertime and the organic hot dogs. A trip to Las Vegas would cut into our summer hang, which I'd come to idealize. It's complicated, raising a kid who is half Anhedonian. There's always the question of assimilation in this country: How much of your native culture do you keep, and how much do you give up? I wanted her to respect both sides of her heritage, so in the summer I'd teach her how to be a carefree American. We'd sip plus-size colas, watch TV on sunny days, be the lazy assholes the Founders intended.

Then the editor of the magazine asked, What if we

staked you to play in the World Series and you wrote about that?

I had no choice. The only problem was that I had no casino tournament experience.

I'd been playing penny poker since college. College kids counting out chips into even stacks, opening a case of brew, busting out real-man cigars—these were the sacred props of manhood, and we were chronically low on proof. A couple of years later, in the '90s, I had a weekly game. Inconceivable now: getting half a dozen people in the same room every Sunday night. We put in our measly five bucks. There was always someone who'd mined their couch or plundered their jar of laundry quarters, the twenty-something version of hocking your engagement ring.

We talked a lot about who we wanted to be, because we weren't those people yet, and reinforcing one another's delusions took the edge off. You humor my bat-shit novel idea, and I'll nod thoughtfully at your insipid screenplay treatment, or plan for the paradigm-shifting CD-ROM game. Like I said, it was the '90s. Dealer's choice: Everyone got their turn to pick the game and expound upon the next harebrained scheme that would make us artists. The home game is always a refuge from the world. That '90s game was an escape from our unrealized ambitions. We were true gamblers, laundry money or no, because we were sure that if we pulled it off, everything would be different. We were so busy bucking each other up that we barely noticed when someone introduced Hold'em into our mix of Seven Card Stud, Five Card Draw, and Anaconda.

A couple of years after that game trailed off, we started a Brooklyn writers game. A cliché, yes: more props. Monthly, 'cause who had the time now that we were actually writing books instead of just talking about it. The stakes stayed the same, though—five bucks, because we were writers. The game still a refuge, this time from the truth we'd discovered about fulfilling your dreams. We had done it, and we were still the same people. Nothing had changed.

....

There was a brief period, during my '90s game, when I wanted to learn more about poker. I was sick of hanging around doomed hands like a dope, waiting to fill in my straight, hoping that the final down card in Seven Card Stud would paint in my flush. Slow learner that I am, I'd just outgrown pining over women who weren't interested in me, and whenever I looked at a busted hand, it gave me a familiar pathetic feeling. Gamblers and the lovesick want to bend reality. But it's never going to happen. If you woke the hell up, you'd understand that and stop chasing.

It occurred to me that I should research how often

big hands popped up. Full houses and trips and what have you. Not the "odds" of them appearing, as that sounded too much like arithmetic. Just a loose idea of how often nice cards appeared in my hand. So on Sunday afternoons while the hangover matinee played on the TV, I squatted on the floor and dealt out Seven Card Stud for myself and three ghost players. I'd play my game, fill in the dummy hands, and see who'd win.

Did my yearnings pay off—did that Jack appear when I needed it, that scrawny pair bulk up into trips? Well. It wasn't very scientific. Anybody who retained a little high-school math could arrive at the real odds more efficiently. And a couple of rounds for a couple of hours on a couple of Sundays was nothing compared to the weekend crash courses possible during the heyday of online play, when you'd hunker for hours, you got your mouse in one hand and a sporkful of kale salad in the other. But in my little way, I got an intuitive instruction on different hands. At the very least, I stopped chasing straights as much, and that, coupled with my poker mask, paid for some cab rides home Sunday night.

Most poker books include glossaries of poker terms and a list of hand rankings, regardless of the ability level of their target audience. That cardplayer optimism about the Big Score, the one that will Change It All, channeled into crossover dreams, even though nobody knows what the hell they're talking about. In this chapter I'll stop to

♦

define some poker lingo here and there, and will now commence with the requisite breakdown of hand rankings, even though I have no idea what the hell I'm talking about.

For those who have never played, there are plenty of mnemonic devices for remembering the hand rankings, which is really a list of reverse frequency. Some of the tricks—"High pair in your holster, break out the prairie oysters!" and "Full House sends you All-In! Too bad we haven't invented penicillin!"—date to the early frontier days of the game and haven't aged well. It's important to find the rhetorical system that works for you.

In explaining the game to a contemporary American audience, one should employ analogies appropriate to the culture. To start, when judging a five-card hand of random crap, the **highest card** determines its value. No trips, no straights, nothing but, say, a Jack or a King. You got zip. By an American standard of success you've totally botched it. Your worldly possessions—what you've been dealt—are nothing more than a cracked snow globe, a ball of twine, an unwrapped candy cane, the electronic keycard to a job you got fired from six years ago, and a thimble. In a showdown with the Lady with the Crimson Hair, she turns over the same first four items, but instead of a thimble, she has a signed head shot of Ben Vereen. You both have terrible hands, but in a war of who has the better crap, the Lady wins for possessing the highest value item: the Ben Vereen commemorative.

Whoever has the better stuff wins. Sound familiar, American lackeys of late-stage capitalism? After highest card comes **one pair**. You have one Queen, but your opponent has two Queens. Who wins? Imagine the Queens are gas-guzzling sport-utility vehicles. DVD players for the kids, butt warmers, GPS voiced by Helen Mirren. Your family has one SUV, but Big Mitch next door has two of them. Who wins? Exactly. That's the virtue of culturally appropriate mnemonics.

Next comes **two pair**. You have one pair of thermal socks. Ready to throw down with Old Man Winter, "To Build a Fire"–style. Robotron over there has one pair of Miles Davis CDs and one pair of coupons for free Jazzercise lessons. He wins: two pair beats having one pair. Now let's say you also have a pair of *Golden Girls* box sets, so that you both have two pair. The highest value pair determines who wins. In this case, Miles Davis takes it for Robotron. In a face-off between your possibly lifesaving footwear, plus the entire run of a series about the twilight years of four feisty gals, and your opponent's late-period Miles and cardio-heavy Jazzercise, he has the nuts.

Three of a kind, or trips, is best illustrated by a quote from the inspiring story of a young immigrant's pursuit of the American dream, Oliver Stone's *Scarface* (1983): "In this country, you gotta make the money first. Then when you get the money, you get the power. Then when you get the power, you get the women." I know it's a universal quote, speaking to all walks of life, as I've heard suburban white guys cite it without irony. Money, power, women: That's three Aces in your hand right there. Certainly beats what you're usually holding in your hand, boys.

As an Anhedonian, those analogies don't speak to me. What do I see when I'm dealt a **straight**—five cards in a series, like 5-6-7-8-9, not all of the same suit? To my tribe, that's five misfortunes in a row, but not the *same brand* of misfortune. Let's say one afternoon, one after the other in sequence, you: forget the name of someone you've met several times; e-mail an important document late; require an emergency root canal; overcook the risotto; and pick an argument with your partner because you blame them for everything that happened today. That's five misfortunes, but a mix of social, professional, and health-related misfortunes. They are "differently suited."

A **flush** would be five misfortunes of the same kind, or suit. Social, for example. You forget the name of someone you've met several times, pick a fight with a loved one, disrespect a member of the service industry, accidentally cuss during the kid's playdate, and fart loudly during the toast at your cousin's wedding. Fan out these things before you, arrange them by type: They are all in the same family of social disaster, the same suit. Let's say five spades, because you're always digging yourself into a hole.

With a **full house**, we're back to Western measures. A full house is empire-building, conspicuous consumption: a pair *and* three of a kind. And **four of a kind**, say four Aces? First you get the money, then you get the power, then you get the women, then you get a really great deal on a time-share.

The highest ranked hand in poker is the **straight flush**. It's the least likely hand you'll be dealt, rare as a true catastrophe. Like, five health-related disasters, one after the other. That's being stabbed by a hobo with a penknife, an infected hangnail, ashy elbows, tummy trouble from "three-times washed" greens only washed twice, topped off by double stigmata. A real straight flush of bodily complaint. A sign from above.

....

HOLLYWOODING: Using all your years of deceiving others to put on a show at the table. Ever said, "Cute baby," about some newborn who'd found a portal between their Hell Dimension and our world? You may have a career in poker.

....

Playing dummy hands on the living-room floor. But who among us has not played out demented scenes on a dirty carpet? That was basically my entire twenties in a nutshell. Sure, I lived one block up from crack houses, black plastic bags twisting on the bare branches outside, but my pastime acquainted me with some of the hidden physics of the game. I'd have to go beyond my mad-scientist experiments now that I was going to Vegas. I was soft.

I ordered books, the website's previous customers serving up recs via algorithm. *No Limit Hold 'em: Theory and Practice* by David Sklansky and Ed Miller, and the morbidly titled *Kill Phil: The Fast Track to Success in No-Limit Hold 'Em Poker Tournaments* and *Kill Everyone: Advanced Strategies for No-Limit Hold 'Em Poker Tournaments and Sit-n-Go's*. Didn't get too far into the *Kill* books, but I admired the authors for their ambition, after they'd set their sights too low with the first volume.

I'd flipped through Sklansky's famous *The Theory of Poker* some fifteen years earlier. Sklansky was one of poker's philosopher-kings, and wrote the first book on Hold'em in 1976. Smiling in his author photo, with his receding hairline, trimmed beard, and oversize specs, here was the face of a player who knew the holy probabilities, the math teacher come at last to explain the numbers. Sklansky's prose was cool, exact. I had no idea what the hell he was talking about.

Not that it would have helped in my '90s home game that much—our trash, wild-card games spoiled any aspirations of rigor. Poring through this new, Big-Boy Sklansky years later, I felt invigorated underlining phrases such as "Winning the battle of mistakes means making sure that your opponents make frequent and more costly mistakes than you do." The Battle of Mistakes. It sounded like commentary on life in the big city, where sometimes good fortune is just having fewer messed-up things happening to you.

My friend Nathan hosted a one-off game, twenty whole bucks to buy in. Figured I'd employ my new expertise, even if it was only a few chapters' worth. I was pretty high on my assignment. It'd be like one of those pieces where someone does a thing for a year and then writes about it, like cook a classic Julia Child recipe every day, or follow the Bible to the letter, or re-create Ted Bundy's notorious spree with "special noogies" in lieu of murder and whatnot. But instead of one year, it would be two months, because of time constraints and my short attention span on account of the internet. Occasional Dispatches from the Republic of Anhedonia. *Eat, Pray, Love* for depressed shut-ins. Energized for Nathan's game, I'd bust out some crazy Sklansky-Fu on these knuckleheads.

It was the most money I'd ever lost in a home game. The gathering was civilized enough. We shared a profession, all writers of one sort or another, five men and three women. More poets than usual (one), perhaps the circus was in town. Home games, you generally play with your own kind. Every night, all over the country, CPAs

◆

were playing with CPAs, firemen with firemen. You've been driven to the sanctuary of the card table by the same forces. It helps if you have something in common, and this night we warmed our hands by the fires of our undying grievance and anxiety.

The spread was top notch. Sliced meat that came from European pigs that seemed to have succulent body parts American pigs didn't. We ordered fancy pizzas and Middle Eastern food, drank small-batch bourbon and local vodka fermented from stuff pulled from the Gowanus Canal or something, it was hard to read the label. Good to see everybody. We talked apartments (one bedroom or two), kids (one child or two), work travel to boondoggle festivals in exotic lands, teaching gigs in Podunk college towns. The music was niche indie: Everyone kept asking "Who's this," "Who's this," and then the creator of the playlist expounded. And hand after hand, I lost.

The pleasant tableau described above is what a home game is all about. It's not what a casino game is about. That night I played as if those guys knew what I meant by wagering 2.5 times the Big Blind here, betting half the pot on the Turn there. Sklansky, Sklansky, I tried, brother. But what use is my semi-bluff when my nonfiction-writing friend blindly threw chips into the pot, more intent on sharing his story of how his eczema was "really flaring up." His doctors wrote a scrip for a new topical steroid, what the heck, he'll try anything at this point. Sklansky, Sklansky, tell me: How can "The Hammer of Future Betting" pierce the armor plate of "Level with me, guys. How old is 'too old' for breast-feeding?" I was being outwitted by allergies. "You wouldn't think it, but there are some not-bad gluten-free beers on the market. It's my turn? Sure, I'll throw in two bucks. See, instead of using hops . . ." If no one's paying attention to my new, hot-rod playing strategy, does it even exist?

No. I bought in for another twenty, and then another.

They weren't going to drop, these romantics. In love with the final card, the River. They will stay in to see the River, for it will save them, always, plug the holes in the straight, gussy a pair of 5s into trips, reverse the evening's bad luck. The River will wash away their sins, of which they have many: holding on to cards that are real long shots to improve (I'd never do that); ignoring ominous developments on the board and textbook-strong betting from across the table (i.e., from me); and ruining the night of a pal who is stressed out about going to the World Series of Poker and could use a break (me again). My twenty-five-year-old self would've been broken by the losses. A hundred and forty bucks was everything back then. It was beer, cable, and cigarettes. Hope.

That's why serious poker players deride low-stakes limit games as No Fold'em Hold'em, like cineastes sneering at the latest *Texas Chainsaw* retread. This is not art but a massacre of all that is holy. The com-

♦

mon folk, they like their cheap entertainment, play for social currency more than cold hard cash. Tomorrow it's back to filing the quarterly reports, that conference with Kaitlyn's teacher about her absences, getting the boiler checked out. But tonight you are free. You dragged your sorry ass out to forget your daily disasters. Why let an obvious flush muck your hand when the River is going to abracadabra your two pair into a full house? It's fifty cents, it's four more bucks, whatever, to see that last card. Just wanna have some brews and try out that new joke you heard at work, not conform to some Sklanskian ideal of the Game.

Yes, it was everybody else's fault. Not mine for letting these fools draw out on me, for making it cheap to call my bets, for not changing gears to adjust to a loose game. For not realizing the simple fact that a money game is not a tournament. It was like writing short stories and thinking it was the same thing as writing a novel. That night I started sleeping more poorly than usual.

....

YHS: "Your hand sucks," from online play. You post the breakdown of a hand to get advice from the community, but your cards are so bad the situation is a no-brainer. "YHS, moron," is the response that pops up in the chat box. If that's too hard to remember, think of it as "Your

High School." Surely you've not forgotten that particular awfulness.

....

Memorial Day Weekend. Six weeks until the start of the Main Event.

Saturday morning, the Tropicana Poker Room was a whisper. The players were still bent over their late breakfasts, chewing over last night's losses and delivering sure-thing declarations of today's successes. One last, shallow interaction with non-poker-playing companions before everyone diverged to their chosen gambling arena.

In those other quicksand places—beeping and blinking slot sinks, blackjack maws, and overpriced buffets—the casino makes its daily bread. The poker room is a loss leader. That precious square footage eats up room that could be used for any number of more devious money-sucking machines. The house takes a rake, a tiny percentage of each pot, but that's it. Caesars, the Trump Taj Mahal, and all the other casinos sticking up out of the boardwalk like rotten teeth, they host a couple of tournaments a day. Morning, afternoon, evening, recouping the operating expenses (electricity, staff, the inhibition-lowering mist dispersed into the ventilation system) from rooms, meals. The various acts of larceny perpetrated upon the poker players' companions.

♦

For my part, I was not enthused about reading a poker how-to while queued for the omelet station of the buffet. Might as well get caught highlighting *Beyond First Base: Advanced Booby Tips of the Pros* on the way to the prom. I grabbed a grande coffee and performed some last-minute cramming in my room. I was only a third of the way through my tournament primer. It would have to do.

While today was my first casino tournament, I'd played in half a dozen homegrown ones over the years. Once at a bachelor party. At a pal's house once or twice someone had suggested an impromptu tournament, everyone bought in. Unaccustomed to the new pace, folks busted out quickly and pouted on the sidelines, so we gave everybody their money back and started playing Omaha again. One time a friend of a friend organized an eighty-man tournament. He cleared out the desks in his office—some sort of internet boondoggle or design studio—to make room for rented chairs and tables. It was all guys, a real sausage party when we lined up for our table draws, sweating testosterone, trying to figure out who in the room was a chump or a ringer. Was this the set of a gang bang? Gang-bang shoots probably have beer and pizza, too.

I usually ended up placing in the top tier in these scrabbly events, despite my ignorance of tournament physics. The half-dead thing. Today the Trop would show me the real deal beyond those earlier ramshackle affairs.

Before the Feds' crackdown, I would have been practicing on the internet, on PokerStars or Full Tilt, Robotroning through tournament after tournament. Online poker was like one of those "learning helmets" in sci-fi movies, where you plop it in your head and download the knowledge of a dead civilization in, like, five minutes. I had to do it the old-fashioned way, with my pants on.

A few money games chugged along around the tournament tables, which sat like lonely atolls, empty save for their tiny columns of chips. The floor manager chatted with a dealer. I asked him how many people usually signed up for a weekend tourney. He surveyed the quiet room. "Depends." He directed me to the Cage, where the cashiers transacted through barred windows, safe as bodega guys dealing cigarettes and Similac through Plexiglas boxes.

The tournaments I sampled in AC that spring ranged from fifty to a hundred and fifty bucks. Not bad for a couple of hours' escape from one's troubles, plus free booze. The Tropicana morning game cost sixty-two bucks. Fifty went to the prize money, and twelve went to the house. I saw where the twelve bucks was going: to pay for plastic name tags for the dealers and "flesh"-colored hose for the post-nubile cocktail waitresses, who slipped between the tables offering "BAVERGES." It was unclear whether BAVERGES was a question or a command.

Depends was right: only eighteen people signed up

♦

41

♠

that morning. Of course I'd picked a bum game for my first outing; most of my later training missions would have fifty or sixty entrants. There were ten seats at each table, your draw noted on the registration card. I was the first arrival, counting down to my seat number clockwise from the dealer.

"Here?"

"There."

I murmured Starting Hands to myself, the hierarchy of the two cards you are dealt before the flop: JJ can get you into trouble, play 88 in middle position, mess with suited connectors if I was feeling fancy in late position. Despite my trepidation, I wanted to be tested, wanted adversaries unshackled from the gladiator pit beneath the Poker Room—grim Moors, dour Phoenicians, battle-scarred Russell Crowes. Instead I was joined by big-mouth Big Mitches down for the Memorial Day weekend with the missus, a single Robotron initiating search-and-destroy subroutines behind his glasses, and two Methy Mikes, both with a felonious air and a desiccated mien, probably killing time until the cockfight.

For our sixty-two dollars, we received $10K in chips, motley colored. In a tournament there's no correlation between the money you give the Cage dwellers and the number of chips you get, which are really just arbitrarily designated pieces of germ-covered plastic. Every poker room had worked out their turnover rate, of how many starting chips will get the players out in time for the next tournament and make room for the night players. In the World Series of Poker, I'd receive a neat stack of $30K in chips for the $10,000 entrance fee the magazine was ponying up for me. Eventually I'd have to wrap my head around that ludicrous jump in magnitude, but today just playing a whole tournament was enough.

....

POKER GODS: Those entities who watch over your poker existence, engineering deep cashes, bad beats, poor position, crappy players to fleece. An eccentric pantheon, to be sure. Among them, Barda the Two-Faced, who reminds you about that morning meeting, but then fills the gutshot straight in your hand, whereupon you keep losing for another two hours. Don of a Thousand Brain Farts sprinkles magic dust in your eyes so that you bet a flush that is really, really not there. And Tim Old Spice, who is probably responsible for much of the "God is dead" talk the last two centuries. He's in charge of making sure the mouth breather next to you is wearing deodorant. Bit of a slacker.

....

And so it began! With luck I'd get in a few hours of play. In contrast to a tournament, a money table possesses an unpredictable life-span, like a fad diet or a good mood.

♦

After collecting a critical mass of waiting-list hopefuls, the floor manager gives the signal, and then the cash game waxes and wanes as players join, split for the sports book or mani appointment or face time with the wife, lose their roll, or somehow muster the willpower to quit while they're ahead. Late night, when the cards get hazy, the sensible head back to the room, and drunks sit down with pros who have gotten out of bed at 3:00 a.m. so they can feast on these boozy losers. Weekly runs at a $30/$60 table can subsidize Little Gary's orthodontia. Then the table dies, and the process starts again. It's a dry riverbed in the desert, quickened by a sudden cloudburst into brief life before the heat decimates it again.

In a tournament, you play to the last man or woman sitting. Here's how it works:

We get our starter stacks, and then the clock begins. I'd never noticed the TV screens on my previous casino visits, but here they were, on tripods, mounted to the wall, counting down tournament time and stats: six minutes to the next increase in blinds, one hour to the next rest break, here's how many players still survive. Because every twenty minutes or so, the blinds (the initial forced bets) increase. At the start, the Big and Small Blinds were $25 and $25. After twenty minutes, the dealer or floor guy announced the increase, and they became $25 and $50, then $50 and $100, and so on.

After a couple of levels we got a ten-minute rest

break. The tables cleared and Big Mitch hightailed it to the bathroom for a meditation over the urinal abyss. (Why did Kaitlyn have to call our weekend getaway "CialisFest"? Makes me feel kind of low.) The Methy Mikes split to the boardwalk for sunlight and a smoke. The mercury bobbed in the eighties, the first hot weekend after a mean winter and tepid spring.

BAVERGES!

I declined. On breaks I parked myself at a one-armed bandit. Out of sight of the Poker Room, scanning my poker tips. "Play the cards they have," my notes said, "not the cards you want them to have." Don't get all starry-eyed and ignore what the cards are saying just because you like the flop. "Are Ace-Jack suited really worth risking your tournament life???" Underlined, starred in the margin, circled in unignorable loops. I don't know how "STAY SEXY" snuck in there, but I nodded thoughtfully.

After the break, I measured my stack against the rest of the table: Well, that guy over there is fairly crippled, I'm not the worst here. Then steeled myself for the next round of meat-grinder levels. My notebook had one voice, encouraging and handing out sticker-stars of achievement like a second-grade teacher, but my stack spoke in a different register: "You better step up, son." The chips, the chips wouldn't shut up, a One Ring hectoring my hunched Gollum self.

◆

"Whoever invented poker was bright," the saying goes, "but whoever invented chips was genius." Uncouple cash money from its conventional associations, and people gamble more freely. Sure, green cash is already a metaphor, but the real pain of seeing actual money disappear into a lost pot is not. No longer milk, meat, and rent, the plastic tokens are tiny slivers chipped off an abstraction, an index of two things: Time and Power.

Obviously, the more chips you have, the longer you can play. But a tournament has more hyperinflation than a CIA-toppled banana republic. As in real life, chips don't buy as much as they used to as time goes by. The blinds are escalating every level—$300 and $600, $500 and $1,000 blinds, $3,000 and $6,000. Your stack becomes more worthless every hand. The more chips you accumulate, the more Time you have left. At the final WSOP table in 2010, the chip leader had $65 million in chips. What is that in Time? Empires rise and fall in that interval. That's glacier time, Ice Age time, knuckle-dragger into Neanderthal time.

And Power. That tower of chips you've made, looming over the rim of the table, is the physical manifestation of how much you can bully. A monument to your prowess, or the Poker Gods' blessing this day. Big stacks eat little stacks like M&M's. The other saps have arranged their stacks into houses of straw and sticks, and even the brick ones will not stand at your re-raise huffing and puffing. What threat is that little stack's All In to someone who'd gathered a thousand times as many chips? I'd always marveled at the gravity-defying properties of those gigantic stacks. Aren't they afraid of knocking them over? My anxiety-palsied hands would send them flying through space. But the first step to handling chip castles is accumulating a bunch of chips, hence my lack of practice.

So: Gather a big stack and people won't want to tangle with your King Kong self. On the Simian Scale, I was more Bubbles the chimp, break-dancing for cigarette and gin money before Michael Jackson rescued him from the streets. Hanging on, overcautious. An early misstep set me brooding. I was Big Blind, with a 9 and a 7, differently suited. Crap, but my forced ante dragged me into the flop—where a pair of 7s gave me trips. Cool. But this young madman in middle position called with 8-7 offsuit (Why was he in? Why, why?) and took the pot with a full house. I lost half my stack. Shut me up for a while.

As it turned out, one aspect of my personality would help me in my odyssey: I was a bider. Temperamentally suited to hold out for good cards, well accustomed to waiting. We Anhedonians have adapted to long periods between good news. Our national animal is the hope camel. We have no national bird. All the birds are dead.

Hyper-aggressive play—taking any two starting hands and rigging some MacGyver-type hand-winning apparatus out of them—was beyond me this early in my training. But in a tournament, you can go hours without decent opening cards. Even an aggressive player only plays four hands out of ten. Everyone, from these weekend plodders in the Trop Poker Room to the seasoned players I'd play with in Las Vegas, had to learn to suffer a rough table, a short stack, some weird hex your next-door neighbor put on you for playing polka music too loud. You bide. Pray. Try to keep cool. Eventually the cards will come. The biding, spider part of me thrived in tournaments.

But biding only gets you so far in poker. Just partway through my strategy manual, and I was already becoming aware of different phases in the game. In the coming weeks, I'd watch the tournaments disintegrate. Forty-eight, thirty-two, sixteen players left. A stickler will shout "Hank! You gonna break this table?" and Hank the floor manager takes a gander. We get chip racks, rack 'em up, and move to our new station. The tables broke and we hopped to the next one as if scampering across splintering ice floes. A broken table exiled opponents to the other side of the room, and then another returned them. Or didn't. They prospered in that new land, or withered, and the story of their table journey merged with mine to create this afternoon's epic. When tables drop to five or six players, the manager reassigns players to maintain distribution, because the game changes depending on how many people are seated. Like, flopping a high pair isn't that great when you're ten-handed—there are too many people who might have better cards. But it ain't bad against six players, and heads up against one player, it's awesome.

At the Final Table, there's nothing left to break. Last man standing.

·········

WORST DAY OF THE YEAR: The day you bust out of the World Series of Poker.

·········

I made it to my tournament's Final Table with a minuscule stack. Not that "Final Table" meant much when there were only two tables to begin with. The Methy Mikes were reunited, sweeping their long stringy hair out of their faces between hands. They'd taken damage, too. Also present: two fellows who didn't fit the demographic of my first table. One was a young Middle Eastern man in his early twenties, dressed in stylish, slim-cut clothes, who mixed it up affably, knocking down hands. He was no Robotron, or if he had been at one time, he'd gotten some back-alley doctor to remove his implants. His girl-friend dragged over a chair and sat behind him sipping a cocktail. She didn't mind waiting, and ignored the guy on her boyfriend's right who kept hitting on her. When the Lothario busted out, they chuckled.

The other castaway was an elderly white man who bent over his chips, squinting through a magnifying attachment that barnacled on his thick specs like a jeweler's loupe. He pondered before acting, as if reviewing a lifetime of hands and confrontations, or fighting off a nap. Sometimes you have to accept a casino trip for what it really is: an opportunity to see old people. There were a lot of old people in poker rooms, genially buying in for a couple of hands before the Early Bird Special. I prefer to believe they were gambling with discretionary funds, enjoying their twilight years after a lifetime of careful saving, and not pissing away their Social Security. If I were an octogenarian looking for love, I'd hit the casinos, no question. The dating pool is quite deep.

The atmosphere at the Final Table was different. Never fast-moving, today's game decelerated even more. Previously aggressive opponents tempered their play. Something was going on, but I couldn't see it. I'd leave the Tropicana with clues, courtesy of the Methy Mikes. They'd complained all day, first about the paltry turnout ("I bet Caesars is hopping"), and then about how long the game was taking. Only eighteen people, but we dragged on. Maybe the slow levels were cutting into their cockfight prep time, Hercules always requiring a good menthol rub before a bout.

"Waiting for him to push," said one, sourly.

He kept at it. After a few hands, I realized he was talking about me. The dismissive gesture in my direction tipped me off. I hadn't been glared at with such hate by two people since couples therapy. Unfortunately, I had no idea what "pushing" meant.

The next day I'd google it: going All In. But why did he care that I wasn't shoving? Because I had no choice at that point. The Big Blind was $3,000, and I had $9,000. I could survive three rounds. But wait—the Small Blind was $1,500, so I didn't even have that long ($1,500 + $3,000 means it cost $4,500 to play one round, or half my stack of $9,000). Not enough to slow-play or wait for a premium hand. To value bet, not that I knew what value betting was. All I could do was push my cards into the middle and hope that the Hungry Hippos had worse cards. Pushin'. I should have started pushing levels ago, before I got into this deplorable situation. Methy Mike was trying to wrap things up, and there I was sitting like a chump, waiting for a bus that wasn't going to come.

I wanted to say, "Look, I'm on a journey here," but that had never worked except that one time in T.G.I. Friday's and all it got me was a half-off coupon for jalapeño poppers. Methy, I wasn't happy with my paltry chips, either.

♦

I was shocked that I'd survived this far. Tremor in my hands whenever I reached for my stack. I petted the notebook in my pocket for comfort, as if I could absorb my instructions through fabric. Which might appear onanistic to the other players and throw them off their game.

So it felt good when I pushed, ignorance aside, and took my critic out with a flush. Cock-a-doodle-doo, motherfucker. I think it was a flush. My notes say, "gamey tooth, itchy eyeballs, heart palpitations, necrotic finger, incipient flatulence." Five of the same suit.

From there I ran hot, nice cards emboldening me. Last-chancers were swallowed by behemoths. Ill-advised All Ins staggered away, sometimes saying goodbye and sometimes without a word, to hit the bar, to shower before the night out and salvage something from the last few hours of the trip. I had a scheme to disable a Robotron by asking him to calculate pi to the last digit, but he busted before I had a chance. I assembled a nice stack and came in third place. Up $175. The old white guy was second. The last few levels, he'd taken a shine to me, asking me to describe the board when the cards showed up fuzzy in his magnifying lenses. First place was the young dandy, who was now free to rest up before nighttime bottle service with his girlfriend at The Pool over at Harrah's, or the Borgata's MIXX. We were an unlikely Mod Squad, case cracked. I celebrated with some dumplings at P. F. Chang's and caught a bus home.

God doesn't play dice with the universe, but sometimes he plays just the tip. My win was beginner's luck, that freaking bane of poker players everywhere. You welcome some newbie who thinks it "might be fun" to play, what larks, and they take down pot after pot. It's a friendly game, or else you'd beat them senseless. I imagine it's like when you toss a one-legged duck into a *palenque* (Mexican cockfighting arena) and the duck somehow pecks the shit out of all comers. Throws off the natural order.

A certain stinginess with myself, the biding thing, meant I had natural facility with drawn-out contests. There were nameless forces at work in a tourney, however, invisible energies I was just beginning to understand. I wasn't good at asking for help. We go solo, my kinfolk and I, taking each day as an IKEA bookcase we build alone, sans instructions. The leftover pieces? We gobble them down, and sometimes it's the only thing we eat all day.

But I was heading out into the desert, and I couldn't do it alone.

THE
POKER CHIPS
IS FILTH

T he World Series of Poker. My intro to the world of high-stakes competition. I'd never been much of an athlete, due to a physical condition I'd had since birth (unathleticism). Perhaps if there were a sport centered around lying on your couch in a neurotic stupor all day, I'd take an interest. I attacked my training on three fronts:

MENTAL

PHYSICAL

EXISTENTIAL

....

MENTAL: Obviously, I had to improve my game. Like all wretches suddenly called up to the Big Time, I needed

♦

a Burgess Meredith, but good. One who wouldn't scoff at the five-dollar buy-in of my usual game.

. . . Although in the end it was my monthly game that led me to my sensei. After stewing for weeks, I came out to my gang about my Vegas trip. They were excited for me, which expanded the field of my anxiety. It was one thing to bring shame upon myself. That was my occupation. But to let down the crew? Sending an emissary to the World Series was a hallowed home-game tradition. In Anchorage, St. Louis, and Boogie-down Boca, tribes of home players stuffed money in the kitty all year to subsidize a member's entry to the Main Event. The rest maybe flying out for moral support, lap dances, a stint or two in the poker room between railing. My own crew wasn't coming out west, but I'd have to account for myself on return.

Hannah, a recent addition to our writers game, told me about a friend who'd played in the WSOP. Maybe she was worth talking to?

And so, Coach. I met Helen Ellis in a restaurant off Union Square. We shook hands by the hostess station. Underneath her bob of black hair, Helen's mischievous eyes sized me up as if I were a new addition to a cash game. Marking off boxes in a mental Rube/Not Rube quiz. Air of Vulnerability: Check. Whiff of Flop Sweat: Check.

The Alabama in her voice was strong. She'd made no

effort to shed her Southern accent during her time in the city. I respected that, as I'd worked hard over the years to flatten my Anhedonian accent, which one linguist memorably described as "like a flock of geese getting beaten by tire irons."

At cards, when asked what she does for a living, Helen says, "Housewife." Like me, she had her mask. I had my half-dead mug, behind which . . . well, not much was going on, really. Dust Bunny Dance Party. But Helen's hid her poker kung fu, and her deception was a collaboration. In a male-dominated game, where female players often affect an Annie Oakley tomboy thing to fit in, the housewife-player was an unlikely sight. "I get ma'amed a lot." The dudes flirted and condescended, and then this prim creature in a black sweater and pearls walloped them. "A lot of people don't think women will bluff," Helen said. She was bluffing the moment she walked into the room.

Helen started playing in casinos on her twenty-first birthday. Her father met her in Vegas. At midnight he took her to the front of Caesars, with its soaring plaster temples and gargantuan toga'd figures, den of Roman kitsch. Up and down Las Vegas Boulevard, the huge casinos beckoned. "Sit down and look around," Papa Ellis instructed. "This is the Center of the Universe." Helen started playing in the Mississippi casinos close to her home in Tuscaloosa, and when we met she was hitting eight tournaments a year. Biloxi, AC. When it worked out, father and daughter met on the circuit. Husband Lex came, too. He plays a solid game, she said.

Later, I'd see her maintain an imperturbable poker face at the table, but that day Helen couldn't help but raise an eyebrow when I divulged my usual stakes. She agreed to give me some crucial pointers. As we waited for our food, I told her about my Tropicana trip, my poker history. Started to say something about "the biding part of me" and its usefulness in tournaments, as "The Biding" was shaping up to be a new favorite in my personal mythology, edging out old standbys like "All This Misery Is Fuel" and "I Think I Would Have Made a Fine Astronaut, Probably."

She was not impressed with my chump idea of the poker trenches. Why would she care about my penny-ante bull? She'd been to the WSOP, for chrissake.

"Sometimes you just run a table," Helen told me, recounting last year's trip, "and I was running every table I was at." She still savored her nice streak in the WSOP Six Handed No-Limit Hold'em event, one of the run-up matches. The World Series of Poker culminates in the Main Event, but in the six weeks leading up to that big megillah, it is what its name implies, a gauntlet of dozens of matches that embody the ever-changing contemporary poker scene. No-Limit Draw Lowball, H.O.R.S.E., Seven Card Razz. Great players are multidisciplinary, but everyone has the little dances they like, their rumbas and funky chickens.

Apart from the money and whatever emotional fulfillment they project onto winning, the various childhood hurts and core sadnesses they briefly silence through victory, the big poker stars are angling for Player of the Year points. POY points quantify how well you do in the various WSOP events, accounting for the size of each field and the amount of the buy-in. Before the Main Event starts, Helen said, you "see players playing, like, two or three hands at once." Events are running all the time, so if you make it to Day 2 of one match and want to enter Day 1 of another, you gotta do some light jogging between ballrooms, mucking in $2,500 Eight-Game Mix so you can catch the next hand of $3,000 No-Limit Hold'em Shootout down the hall.

Helen said she liked "Six Handed." I had no idea what the hell she was talking about. I nodded and chewed. In 2010 Helen made it through the first day of the $5,000 Six Handed No-Limit. When she got her draw for Day 2, the Powers that Be seated her at a Feature Table with the big guns. Feature as in TV cameras. They played "The Star-Spangled Banner," and Helen looked for her seat. "Where is Table 116? There's 114, there's 118, where is it? Oh, it's the Feature Table up on the platform with all the press, all the lights, and all that shit."

Husband Lex snapped a picture of her playing

against poker superstars Phil Ivey and James Aken-head. Ivey was one of the few big-time African Ameri-can pros—actually, the only one I could name. For years now, I'd rooted for him on TV, whenever he popped up on the poker shows my DVR scooped from the deep a.m. darkness. Cool and inscrutable, he was our black heavy-weight, our Leon Sphinx. Hadn't heard of Akenhead. Turned out he was a British player, a young gun who'd made it to the Final Table in 2009. He came in ninth place, and pocketed a million dollars for his exertions.

"It's, as they call it, the Table of Death." She sur-vived the cameras. She knocked Akenhead out of the game, and once Ivey busted, too, they broke the table. Show over. The next time Helen was in Vegas, she passed Akenhead in the hallways of the Rio. "It's like if you had dinner with Obama. You would remember him, but he might not remember you."

Helen came in forty-second place, winning twelve grand. It was her first pilgrimage to the World Series after stepping up her presence on the professional poker circuit the last few years. Poker and housewifery aside, she was also a writer. She left Tuscaloosa to come to New York to study fiction writing at NYU. I picked up her sec-ond book, *The Turning*, thinking it might provide insight into her poker persona. It's about a teenage girl in NYC who discovers she has the power to turn into a cat, indeed belongs to a larger, secret community of people who can turn into cats. There was a gesture toward the poker sub-culture in that premise, and some riffing on transformation into one's true self, the inner becoming the outer. Your daytime life is one reality, and at night, at a poker table, say, you become someone else. Someone with claws.

"I've been playing since I was twenty-one," she said. "And I still have to gather my courage to go and sit down and be there. I like it because you can be anyone you want to be. I can be extremely aggressive. I can be very brave. I can behave in a way that I don't normally behave. Other than writing, it's the only place where I can lose time."

There's more poker in her first book, *Eating the Cheshire Cat*. It follows three young Southern girls who are also in the midst of violent transformation, this time into brutal adulthood. One climactic scene occurs at a poker play-off held at a sorority reunion. The middle-aged former Delta Delta Deltas are all set up for a nice afternoon of Seven Card Stud, unaware that Nicole Hicks, a next-generation Tri Delt, has penciled in her psychotic break for that afternoon. Her butcher knife comes down and "Within a split second, Mrs. Hicks lost her daughter, her nerve, and two-thirds of her right index finger . . . The blood pooled and lifted the Queen of Spades from the table. It slid to the edge, then fell, face first, splat on the beige, velvet-soft, steam-cleaned carpet."

As in most of the poker tales that overwhelmed me during my training, there was a lesson there, but it would take some time for me to decipher it. For now, I went with: You better listen to Coach.

Helen was the perfect teacher, hipping me to the right books (Dan Harrington and Phil Gordon), dispensing the Poker Truths so that they finally penetrated my brain ("This is your mantra: Patience and Position"), and sharing basic tips about daily survival in Las Vegas's Rio Hotel, home to the WSOP since 2005. "Stay on the Ipanema side—the rooms are better." Following an afternoon at the tables, I was supposed to hit the seafood joint just outside the corridor to the convention hall. "Make a reservation," she instructed, in the same tone she used for "Watch out for A-x in middle position."

Those first weeks, when I was trying to supe up my game, she told me about where to play in AC. "The Borgata and Caesars. Yes, the Taj is in *Rounders*, but it is a dump." More important, she kept me from freaking out at the enormity of the task ahead. "You should play some Sit-n-Go's while you're in Atlantic City. You can't win a tournament if you can't win a Sit-n-Go." I nodded. I pretended to know what a Sit-n-Go was, mustering the same facial expression I used when someone said, "We ended up having a good time" or "Then we fell in love." I mentioned the Robotrons, who saw the flop with anything, pocket lint and paper clips. "I love these young players," she laughed. "Give 'em enough rope. Call their craziness when you have a monster."

She'd teach me things. About poker. About life. It'd be like one of those racial harmony movies I never go to see, like *The Blind Side*, where a Southern white lady instructs a weirdo black guy in how to use a fork. Broken barriers. Montage sequences. Golden Globes. But instead of forking up food, I'd be forking up poker knowledge. The way I understood it, from trailers and Oscar telecast montages, the black person teaches the white person something in return. I had no idea what that would be.

....

EXERCISE: Get a Poker Handle. The Old Masters of poker, they had truly awe-inspiring nicknames: Amarillo Slim, Sailor Roberts, Pippi Longstocking. So I got to brainstorming.

The Slouch: I slouched. Rocket Racer: after the Spider-Man nemesis/ally from the '70s, a black guy on a rocket-powered skateboard. It was a multivalent moniker, alluding to my melanin count, my transportation issues, and "rocket" was slang for pocket Aces. "A pair of Aces, you better get ready to race if you want to take the pot from me," he informed the empty room. Five-Dollar Colson: referring, for once, not to my home-game buy-in but to what I'd charge for most acts if I ever started hooking. I sell myself short a lot. Finally, I went with the Unsubscribe Kid. I liked the implied negation of things other humans might enjoy. Now all I had to do was get someone to ask me what my poker nickname was.

....

Pity the poor pilgrim who gets on a Greyhound bus and hears "Everybody's Talkin'" come over the speakers. You are the Midnight Cowboy, extricating yourself painfully from your past, or you are Ratso Rizzo, expiring in the back row, wheezing and unsaved. But I found my seat, settled in with the day trippers, day workers, and hollow-eyed freaks, and got into the new rhythm of my days. "I can't see their faces / only the shadows of their eyes."

It went like this: I'd drop off the kid at school, hop on the subway to the Port Authority, and catch a bus to AC. Then I'd gamble gamble gamble, catch a midnight bus back to the city, sleep all day, and pick up the kid from school the next afternoon. I'd make dinner, put her to bed, read Harrington, take her to school, and start over again.

Over the years, my half-dead face had kept drop-off patter to a minimum, but occasionally I'd share a few words with the other parents on the way into the Lower School.

"Can't believe the school year's almost over."

"They grow up so fast."

"Off to work?"

"Actually, I'm going to Atlantic City to gamble."

I see.

Was there a corresponding decrease in playdates? Sorry, little one. Flushed down to the social sub-sewers with Disgraced Embezzler Dad and Grifter Mom. They were scarce now, those two, at the First-Grade Parents Pot Luck, so I couldn't even swap exile anecdotes with them.

I ran around AC. The all-you-can-eat buffet was central to the American Gambling Experience, allowing you to block your arteries while unstopping your bank account. I applied a philosophy of generous sampling to my casino tours, zipping across downtown in taxis to try the shrimp cocktail at the Borgata, the prime rib that is Caesars, saving a corner on my plate for the pigs in a blanket that characterized the Showboat.

I never lasted long at the Borgata, the biggest and swankiest joint in town, constructed according to prevailing Vegas theories of the megacasino. Leisure Industrial Complex all the way. Just as the cozy old casinos of Frank and Dean were razed to make room for colossal gambling pleasure domes, so was AC being reconfigured for the current needs of the LIC. You can only cram so many buildings on the boardwalk. How are you going to fit that Euro-style spa, TV chefs' small-plate eateries, the vast dance-floor killing fields demanded by international hero-DJs? Hence the twin, shimmering gold towers of the Borgata. Located in the marina area, explaining the establishment's name, which is Esperanto for "built on a swamp."

Coach was right. The 'Gata had the most popular poker room in town, having assumed the mantle from the Trump Taj. The Taj was the home of Hold'em during the late-'90s surge in the game's popularity. The final showdown in the Matt Damon poker vehicle *Rounders* propped up its reputation for a time. Nowadays, online poker forums warned of muggings, shady clientele, and shadier doings. Which wouldn't happen at the Borgata—one whiff of the bewitching aromas from Bobby Flay's grill, and even the most larcenous soul is scared straight by the tang of nouveau Tex-Mex flavor profiles.

On a typical Borgata jaunt, I entered a late-morning tournament, got bounced by noon, and then did a divining-rod thing with my phone to find a signal so I could figure out where to hit next. I'd hear Coach's voice whenever I did this: "Keep that in your pocket." People slouch at the tables, earbudded, listening to whatever, a hundred-song loop of various covers of Kenny Rogers's "The Gambler," from Liza Minnelli's New Wave–inflected version to Lou Reed's unreleased, oddly affecting acoustic demo. No distractions, she said. It took a lot of willpower. I feel about my phone the way horror-movie ventriloquists feel about their dummies: It's smarter than me, better than me, and I will kill anyone who comes between us.

I only conferred with my little buddy between levels, checking advice on poker sites: when do you throw out a probe bet, how much do you bet on the button? I subscribed to the Poker Atlas's Twitter feed, which had the city's tourney schedule on constant scroll. Tackle the 1:00 p.m. Bally's $55 tourney, Harrah's 1:15 p.m. start for $100, or Caesars' 1:15 p.m. dealio, also a hundred bucks? I didn't have intel on which poker rooms were dead or barely twitching. Sometimes there weren't enough players for a game, and I'd hike it back to the marina for a mid-afternoon shift at Harrah's. Sometimes something big was going down, like the World Poker Tour, and there'd be no one to deal because all the dealers were moonlighting across town. These miscalculations cut into my shrinking practice time, already too tight. Where to next, where to next?

....

EXERCISE: Manage tells. Table image is the one-man show you tour through town after town. Every poker player has a shtick, is Hal Holbrook doing *Mark Twain Tonight!* across Podunks. You have heard of the famous "tells"—the behavioral clues that put you onto someone's hand, such as squeezing out armpit farts or crooning "Touch Me in the Morning" when they hit their gutshot straight. I didn't have time to become a master reader of tells, between keeping track of inflection points, calculating rough pot odds, and riffling through my mental catalogue of new poker knowledge. But I could manage my own tells, come up with some fake ones to psyche people out. If I shared them here, you'd know my secrets, but here's a freebie: Reenacting the chest-buster scene from *Alien* means I'm on a draw.

....

There was one establishment in AC that always had a game going. It was never recommended by players I met. Indeed they invariably guffawed at the mention. But the mighty Showboat was always there for me, like a dependable neighborhood bodega. It had what I needed.

My first Showboat experience came after I'd been turned away from a totally dead Caesars card room, which I'd rushed to after getting the boot from a Borgata tourney. The Caesars floor guy told me there weren't going to be enough players. I came down to AC for this? My flop days were adding up, and when I did play, I busted early. I got into a taxi to the bus station . . . and almost made it there before I told the cabbie to turn around. Time to try the Showboat.

If the Borgata served up the contemporary luxury-resort experience, the Showboat specialized in the more particular fetish of nostalgia. The name harkened to the glorious heyday of riverboat gambling, you know, with those steam-powered boats with the big paddlewheels, where ladies with parasols promenaded on deck and men pulled out their watch fobs to see if they had time for "a little game of chance." Pioneers of the casino captive-audience thing. I gather proximity to water was too tempting for despondent gamblers, which led to the rise of the landlocked, more suicide-proof gambling house. The cheap stakes of nickel slots en route to the exit can talk a body off the ledge.

From this antebellum home square, the Showboat hopscotched in and out of decades. The '50s-themed Johnny Rockets burger joint reminded boomers of sock hops, roller-skating waitstaff, the first backseat gropings. The House of Blues served up rootsy sentimentality, reminiscences of swell nights in blues franchises in New Orleans, Houston, San Diego. (Remember those two sloppy German matrons? Too bad we had to get up early the next day for the ConAgra convention.) Yes, Big Mitch, there was a time before second mortgages and leaky roofs and Kaitlyn crashing the car for the second time. The piped-in Nirvana and Pixies—now officially oldies bands—welcomed middle-aged, Gen-X lumps like me. The sights and sounds of bygone days told us that anything was still possible, the way the snap of a dealer cutting cards and the maddening chimes of loose slots assured us we could be winners. That sure, gambling sound of promise.

The Showboat Poker Room was compact but busy, and I'd usually last a few hours among the sad-sack tourists and young, sharp-eyed local talent.

BAVERGES! the cocktail waitresses called.

HARRINGTON! I responded.

His head hovered on the covers of volumes I, II, III like a rheumy-eyed Oz. Eyes peering beneath a green Red Sox cap, observing, judging, as if to ask, "What, actually, are you rooting for on the flop?" and "Why don't you make a standard continuation bet of about half the pot, and see what happens?" Do you have enough outs? Are you discouraging action pre-flop?

Who was this Hold'em sage, this Hoyle-bred Socrates? His name was Dan Harrington and in the early part of the twenty-first century, he published his ridiculously influential, multivolume *Harrington on Hold 'em: Expert Strategy for No-Limit Tournaments*. Every discipline has its master texts. Harrington's books are to boom-era poker players what Sun Tzu's *The Art of War* is to mealy-mouthed I-bankers ("All warfare is based on deception"), as essential as *Speak, Butter* is to artisanal emulsion-makers ("To churn is to live").

Harrington was almost sixty years old when he wrote the first volume. He'd won two WSOP bracelets, cashed millions of dollars, and made it to Main Event Final Table two years in a row, the first player to do so. And possibly the last—the game was undergoing a fundamental shift.

Chris Moneymaker's legendary win in the 2003 Main Event had summoned the amateurs to Vegas, transforming the game in the manner that trimming fat from muscle meat and curing it in the sun turns animal flesh into delicious jerky. Online sites like PokerStars and Ultimate Bet were virtual poker universities, matriculating thousands. The new kids needed passwords to authorize bank transfers, and they needed textbooks. *Harrington on Hold 'em* codified conventional wisdom, elucidated the inner-circle concepts, and helped create a common tournament slang of squeeze plays, inflection points, and M.

Coach gave me Harrington homework, and I made slow but incremental progress through his strategies for satellites, internet tourneys, and brick-and-mortar showdowns. His words yielded new interpretations over time, like a really neat poem or a divorce settlement. I keyed into the rhythms of the game, the phases within phases. There is an early, middle, and late temperament to each tournament, and inside that, an early, middle, and late temperament to each hand. Harrington hipped innocents like me to the late-stage tourney mind-set and late-hand strategies, giving names to that which I understood only on a subconscious level.

Like: Why had play tightened up, slowed down in that first Tropicana tournament? Because even in that shorthanded game, we had approached the Great Membrane of the Bubble. The top 10 percent of players inside the Bubble get a share of the winnings. Everyone wants in after playing for so long, so they get conservative. No one wants to be the "Bubble Boy," the last schnook who gets close and walks away with nothing. Methy Mike had wanted me, and my hanging-by-my-fingertips stack, to hurry and vamoose so the endgame could start.

Usually the prose in poker books is as ugly and utilitarian as their layouts. The Harringtons, while not skimping on the lingo, were furnished with an easy-going inclusive voice. And plenty of work problems. He dropped a bunch of science, then slowed things with study hands that he broke down step by step. "Do you fold, call, or raise?" "What now?" "You should limp into this pot with 3 callers ahead of you in this scenario," he'd instruct—and then go on to describe what happens if you ignored his advice. The annotated blunders were especially helpful. I discovered that whenever I bet horrendously or busted out, it was because I'd strayed from his teachings. *I was the very dumbshit he described!*

But like I said, everyone had read the same book. You knew what they were up to and vice versa. After Doyle Brunson self-published his massive poker bible, *Super System*, in 1978, he lamented giving away his secrets. In the old days, "The top players would let the inferior players round up the money; then they would beat them. The hometown champions would break their local games, then come out [to Vegas] and be broken by us." Then they read Brunson's book of spells and started to beat the pros. "If I had to do it again, I wouldn't write that book."

As the Main Event neared, I binge-watched a bunch of WSOP games from that spring. There was Harrington, pushing away from the table, busted, given a Viking funeral from the on-air commentators. The kids resumed play without him. They had their diplomas.

And they were making new discoveries.

....

EXERCISE: Preserve my "essence." Like heavyweights who refrain from sexual activity prior to a big bout in order to channel and convert that energy into violence, I, too, would safeguard my "essence." The mind-body harmony thing. Then it was brought to my attention that preserving one's "essence" meant no self-abuse. Once again, I had failed myself without even knowing it. Just as I had made a judgment call that I didn't have time to become a maestro in playing suited connectors in middle position, I'd have to forgo this segment of my regimen. Stamp this part of my training REVISED.

....

The dealer tossed the cards around the table. Was there something I was supposed to remember? Right: Patience and Position. I had the first P down, what with the biding, etc., and over the years my day job had strengthened

♦

my natural talent in that area. In novel-writing, biding is everything. How will I drag my mutilated body over the finish line, hundreds of pages later? You practice a slow parceling out of self to survive the swamp of self-doubt, to tolerate the juvenile delinquent sentences who keep acting out. Waiting years for a scofflaw eleven-word sentence to shape up into an upstanding ten-word sentence: This is the essence of Patience.

And what did Coach mean by Position? You are at a poker table. Social dynamics and probabilities change according to how many people you are up against and where you're sitting. Why was Helen's Six Handed game different, why did Heads-Up require its own branch of study? Seriously, there are Heads-Up experts—they have their own NBC-TV show and armbands.

Well, imagine you are alone in a room. The lights are down low, you've got some scented candles going. Soothing New Age tunes, nothing too druid-chanty, seep out of the hi-fi to gently massage your cerebral cortex. Feel good? Are you the best, most special person in the room right now? Yes. That's the gift of being alone.

Then a bozo in a CAT Diesel Power cap barges in. What's the chance that you are the best, most special person in the room now? Fifty-fifty. If you both were dealt two cards, those would be your odds of holding the winning hand.

Now imagine ten people are in the room. It's cramped.

You're elbow to elbow, aerosolized dandruff floats in the air, and the candle's lavender scent is complicated by BO tones, with a tuna sandwich finish. What are the chances you're the best, most special person in the room? If you were handed cards, you might expect to be crowned one time out of ten.

People, as ever, are the problem. The more people there are, the tougher you have it. Just by sitting next to you, they fuck you up, as if life were nothing more than a bus ride to hell (which it is). But what if you moved to another seat? Changed position? Your seat is everything. It can give you room to relax, to contemplate your next move. Or it might instigate your unraveling.

Sometimes you act first. Sometimes last. If you have a small pair and you're under the gun, as they say, how do you know what to bet? Nine intruders are going to act after you, and your big raise might be a mistake. It'd be so nice to wait and see what they were going to do, to kick back and enjoy the scenery before committing. The lady in late position has that luxury of time and space. If four crazies jump in, raising and re-raising and bebopping all over the place, she can politely fold and watch the carnage.

Different hands are more or less playable depending on whether you're the first, middle, or late to act. You'll always play a pair of Aces, but when you're sitting in late position with deuces while Mothra and Godzilla are stomping Tokyo? Hide in the subway tunnels with the other terrified citizens and wait for the sounds of carnage to stop. Pick your fights like you pick your nose: with complete awareness of where you are.

Why was Six Handed different, and why did Helen like it? If you ask me, it's because I'm only competing with five people to be the best, most special person in the room. The more learned among us would say that Six Handed is a different beast because there's more action. Mercenaries like war because they like to scrap it up, and they get paid. More hands per hour at a smaller table, the orbits spinning and spinning, and weaker holdings, like one pair or two pair, become more playable due to less competition. Heads-Up, even more so. Pure combat.

"I'm terrible at the Final Table when it's Heads-Up," I complained to Coach at the end of our first meeting. Dealing one-on-one with another person, in primal communication, it fed my psychological defects. My shrink thought this was a suitable line of inquiry, and perhaps we'd get to it once we dealt with all that other crap.

"You won't be playing Heads-Up," Helen said. In the WSOP, like all tournaments, when people get knocked out the guys on the floor fill the seats with other players, but once the Main Event is reduced to nine guys, they adjourn until November. To maximize TV ratings. In the unlikely event al-Qaeda gunned down everyone in the tournament except for me and a Robotron, I'd have plenty of time to learn about proper Heads-Up play.

The study problems in Phil Gordon's books gave me grief, I told her. "Phil Gordon's always like, 'I was at this table playing 8-6 offsuit'—"

"Forget that. You're too you to play that way. Play your game."

I was too me. Precisely.

....

EXERCISE: Floss. It's difficult not to think about decay in a casino. How all our hopes and dreams are but insubstantial creatures, prey to chance and human frailty. The winnowing of hope, the evanescence of desire. Those horror-show pants we bought that one time. One can't help but contemplate decay when confronted with such a constant parade of monstrous dentition in casinoland. That's what I got for playing the cheapo games, but still, take care of yourselves, people.

....

I threw myself into my training. My game was improving, even if I had yet to repeat the success of my first tournament. It was nice to have a diversion from how I usually spent my days, which was basically me attempting to quantify, to the highest degree of accuracy, the true magnitude of my failures—their mass, volume, and specific gravity. It passed the time in the absence of hobbies. Sure, I worked on my nagging sense of incompleteness a lot, when I had a spare moment, but that was more of a calling than a hobby.

On to the second area of training, *PHYSICAL*:

The vessel of my body—this fragile sack of blood, "essence" (see above), and melancholy humors—had to get up to competition-grade performance. I'd long aspired to the laid-back lifestyle of exhibits at Madame Tussaud's. There are cool perks. You don't have to move around that much or waste energy on fake smiles, and every now and then someone shows up to give you a good dusting. Over time I had indeed become the wax-dummy version of myself, but that wouldn't cut it at the Main Event.

Throughout the ages, much has been written about the interrelatedness of the mind and the body. Suburban moms who lift Volkswagens off pinned toddlers, for example. I'd be a fool to ignore the holistic reality. In Vegas, I'd be lifting metaphorical Kias and Hyundais left and right.

To the outside observer, it seems like poker involves a lot of reclining in chairs, but you're still burning fuel. "Lex and I lost five pounds!" Helen informed me, referring to their last trip. The Main Event at the World Series of Poker ran seven days, each one a twelve-hour series of jungle engagements. You had to be vigilant. You grab a bite when you can, the caloric intake going to power your game, your all-important table image, the mask of your poker identity: alternately representing strength and weakness, riding herd over tells, manufacturing ersatz tells, placing bait for traps, stealing and thieving blinds. Picking up chips. Putting down chips. It adds up.

Could someone gimme a hand in my new self-improvement scheme? Up until now, my idea of "making a new start" was not importing my bookmarks to a new browser. My torpor had stretch marks.

Finally I got a recommendation from an old girl-friend who'd become a physical trainer. I think she and I are in agreement that we were a crappy couple, both of us subprime dating quality, even by the low, low standards of early-'90s High Slackitude. It had been a terrible relationship, but I was grateful, for it prepared me for terrible relationships to come, so that I would not be surprised. The *Matrix* sequels, for example. In later years, she became a physical trainer and left the state. She was very helpful and gave me a local name: Kim Albano.

Kim was a licensed physical trainer and patient soul. A Long Island native, she moved to the city in '99 and entered the biz because she simply loves inspiring people to be healthy. She called her practice "Conscious Intermodel Fitness," specializing in posture and core strengthening, Vinyasa yoga with a little Iyengar thrown in. Alexander Technique. I had been given yoga mats over the years as gifts, but the phrase "loose-fitting clothing" had always confounded me, conjuring visions of tunics or otherwise Jawa-type vestments, neither of which I owned. I ultimately opted for dad-style cargo shorts, whose multiple pockets I increasingly relied on to spare me the indignity of carrying a fanny pack or man bag.

I met Kim at a space she sometimes used on Fourth Avenue in Brooklyn. She'd offered me a group lesson in Prospect Park with some of her regulars. Too public, I thought. I preferred to work out like I eat beef jerky: making vulgar grunting noises sans witnesses. Needless to say, I was a tad let down when the storefront studio allowed passersby to observe my lesson. Another exhibit in the bizarre sideshow that is a New York street. Per usual.

I described my assignment before we met, and she was amenable. "I have to become a Living Poker Weapon in six weeks," I said.

"You mentioned 'Rocky-style' in your e-mail," she said.

"This might be a bit conceptual."

Kim did my intake, quizzing me about my exercise history (mere vapor), ailments (psychosomatic in the main), and hydration regimen ("You have to keep drinking water"). Was I under stress? I had just finished a book, I explained, so I was less stressed than I had been. Any injuries she should be aware of? The only big thing was this formidable crick in my neck, which had only lately disappeared. My magnificent ergonomic chair, the steadfast galleon I had sailed through books and books, had finally sprung a leak. After ten years, the webbing of the seat had given way, so I stuffed a throw pillow in there when I had to work. I sat in there half sunk, arms grotesquely angled, and over the weeks a stupendous crick took up residence around my left shoulder blade. The pain was exacerbated by my habit of crawling to the living-room couch when I had insomnia. The 5:00 a.m. traffic reports on the bleary, early-bird news shows often returned me to sleep—in my aforementioned license-less state, the reports of blocked interstates and impenetrable bridges were a lulling white noise to me, abstractions stripped of meaning. I was sleeping on the couch so much it was as if I were married again. "But it's mostly gone away," I told Kim.

I described an average day at the tournament, the importance of keeping your shit together as you trudged through bad beats and dead cards, resisting the lure of going "on tilt"—a species of berserker rage that destroyed one's game play. She taught me how to sit. She taught me how to breathe according to the basic principles of the nineteenth-century health guru F. M. Alexander, and reintroduced me to my neglected spine, which I had long treated as a kind of hat rack for my sundry, shabby articles of self.

We ran through elementary yoga poses—cat, cow, downward dog. I mentioned that we got twenty-minute breaks every two hours. What could I do to stay loose and limber? She said, "Cat, cow, downward dog." I said, "I can't do that in a casino." My table image would suffer. We proceeded. I liked the sitting and the breathing, the glancing moments of "proprioception."

"Bring it into you," she said, "make it yours, and then you can bring it into your poker."

As I walked out into the glare and early-summer heat of Fourth Avenue, I felt a peculiar sense of well-being, which I quickly banished by sheer force of will, as I didn't want to ruin my streak. Assimilating this knowledge would take time, but I felt that soon I would be a lean, mean sitting machine.

....

EXERCISE: Sunglasses. Like most people, I'd spent my whole life looking for a socially acceptable situation in which I could wear sunglasses indoors, and here it was. They made for good TV, most definitely, the sunglasses guys and their imposing, unreadable faces, their lenses reflecting back your own dumb face. Mirrored, wrap-around, robin's-egg-tinted. Sunglass Hut did not stock what I required. I needed the exactly just-so pair, some sort of Vulcan smithy-god to forge them in the very bowels of the earth, a set of glowing, molten intimidation shades in a scene drawn by Walt Simonson. Well, I tried, but despite my efforts I couldn't bring myself to wear sunglasses during my practice runs. The social taboos were too strong, or my inner douche-bag monitor set too high, I dunno. I'd have to make do with my naturally half-dead mug.

....

Playing cards, making friends. Before one break, the elderly gent next to me told me, "You're a good player."

"Thanks."

What had he seen in his life? A world war, a cold war. Dude walks on the moon, and another invents the internet. After the civil rights movement, the arrival of the first black president, perhaps the early twenty-first-century wonder that is a poker table in a hypermodern casino, and my presence there, reminded him of how much the world had changed in his lifetime.

"But you know what?" he added.

"What?"

"You talk too much!" Cackling.

I kept my mouth shut, it was true. Poker was the perfect game for me, as I didn't have to speak. It was like Disneyland for hermits. I had found the place where I could go out among the humans, elbow to elbow for hours, and not say a fucking word. It brought me back to the old days, when I first started to write, and I'd spend whole days shut up in my apartment and the only thing I'd say to another living being was "... and a pack of Winston Lights."

Quite a few things about poker reminded me of the writing life. Like, you sat on your ass all day. That was a huge one. Big plus. And we were all making up stories, weaving narratives. Pros will talk about "the story you're telling with your hand." A hand possesses a narrative arc with a setup, rising action, denouement. Each time you throw money into the pot you're telling a story, from the opening call to the River re-reraise. As Saint Harrington put it, "A player is nothing more than the sum of his betting patterns." After years of experience, you recognize plots: He must have trips, and that guy's representing a flush by raising the pot on that third heart. You must fake out their reads, misdirect through the red herring of a half-pot bet or a bluff, spinning a story through hours of tells, betting patterns, your poker persona. Until the endgame, when the psychology of the characters catches up with everybody. Always on the lookout for that M. Night Shyamalan twist at the end when you discover you were dead the whole time.

The day-to-day horror of writing gave me a notion of tournament time. Writing novels is tedious. When will this book be finished, when will it reveal its bright and shining true self? It takes freakin' years. At the poker table, you're only playing a fraction of the hands, waiting, ever waiting for your shot. If you keep your wits, can keep from flying apart while those around you are self-destructing, devouring each other, you're halfway there. The poseurs yakety-yaking about the Fitzgeraldian flourishes of their latest novella, the puffed-up middle-managers droning on about how they knew you had 10s—they never make it to the Final Table. Let them flame out while you develop a new relationship to time, and they drift away from the table.

Poker players and writers are always inside the game and also outside the game observing it. When I whipped out my notebook, no one blinked. I could have been recording bad beats, misplayed hands, or assembling a dossier on other players. No one cared what I scribbled. *Like when you write a book.*

....

EXERCISE: Purify the spirit. I had to improve my diet in Vegas, start eating a proper breakfast in order to make it through each day's marathon. "Do you eat meat?" Helen asked. I did. "Good." It was a long time to the dinner break, and that's when some players start drinking, and drinking led to errors. No more ruining my body with noxious substances, poisoning my mind with various toxins. I was doing well with the cigarettes, had been off them for nine months, although it helped that the disappointment of not having a post-dinner cigarette, or a just-stepped-outside cigarette, or a just-woke-up cigarette was dwarfed by the newer, state-of-the-art disappointments the world threw my way. I was saved by scale.

Why stop with cigarettes? I could renounce more things, like (1) cut back on my microbrews and (2) most reality television. Get behind me, master brewers of Brooklyn, Portland, and Chapel Hill, you hipster hopsters and your newfangled brands of incipient, yuppified alcoholism. My reality-TV purge—*America's Got Schlubs, Keep Trying to Outwit Death You Stupid Monkeys*—meant everything save the competitive weight-loss shows, whose contestants, I recognized, were on a parallel journey to my own. *The Biggest Loser*: exactly so. My failures possessed a weight, I carried them around, and before poker I sought the proper instrument of their measure. These reality-TV pilgrims had already learned how to calculate their weakness, for its substance possessed an actual mass determinable before a live TV audience. Those shows made me more teary than Pixar movies, the unalloyed pleasure these guys and gals displayed over their new mastery of self, the erasure of decades of daily, mounting mistakes. Just look at the pants they used to wear. This one guy lost a hundred and fifty pounds and said, "I was carrying another man around." They had found themselves: It had been hiding in their skins all this time, waiting. That better, biding self. I could do it. More fiber, for starters.

Coming back at night was the worst of it. I'd briefly glory over some incremental improvement in my play, then remember I hadn't won any money since my first Trop excursion. So much for aptitude. I was like a piece of meat, hacked from a carcass and heavily spice-rubbed, but still waiting to be smoked. Waiting to become what it was meant to be: a tough, cured, beautiful strand of jerky.

Weeks passed, but my Word-A-Day Calendar was stuck on "motherfucker." At the end of my AC working day, I'd hit the bus terminal, with its wee-hour convocation of squalor. The buses didn't run as frequently at night—it was easier to get in than out. Roach Motel. Drunks, drug-addled denizens, and Those with Nowhere to Go shambled about, trapped in the depot. When the bus finally arrived, the ride back was quiet and dark, the powered-down Port Authority a maze of metal gates and closed-off corridors. The terminal was too sprawling and impossible to police otherwise. Rotten Old New York, the Ratso Rizzo New York was still here. I didn't know what I was doing there. Anyone present at that hour was a clump of hair stuck in the American drain. I just wanted to get home and catch some sleep before I saw the kid.

. . . .

Then I ran out of time. Met with Coach for a final huddle. She'd just returned from the early stage of the WSOP, that land of abundant Omaha Hi-Low and H.O.R.S.E., Six Handed. Trying to scrape up a stake for the Main Event.

"It was heaven. Heaven!" Pure joy in her voice at the thought of it. Although Helen cashed deep in the $1,500 No-Limit event, she didn't win enough to pay her way into the Big Game. She was off gambling until September. "I had an agreement with myself," she said. "That's how we tell ourselves we're not addicts." Whatever works, I say. Since she'd returned east, she'd been too bummed to follow WSOP news. I tried to give her an update, what I had gleaned from her Twitter list of players to follow, but I was pretty useless.

Coach gave me another poker seminar, and I scribbled bullet points. She briefed me on some new moves she hadn't seen before—people in Vegas were breaking out their next-level shit all over the place. After listening to her talk of stealing blinds and short-stack mentality, I was freaking out. Told her so. She shared a new mantra she'd come up with for this last WSOP trip: "It's okay to be scared, but don't play scared." When you're scared, that means you're paying attention. Don't let it destroy you.

I recalled the time my father abandoned me in the Dismal Forest in Northern Anhedonia when I was eight. He blindfolded me, put a crossbow in my hands, and said,

"Don't come back until you take down a twelve-point buck for supper." Was I scared? Sure. But I did what he asked of me, and over the years I'd successfully convinced myself that I was a better man for it. (Never lost my hatred of squirrels, however, the devious little fuckers.) Fear situates you in the moment. Focuses you. I knew that.

"You're gonna be targeted no matter what, 'cause you're very pretty. You do not look like the typical player."

Pretty?

"You know, you got the threads. I have never seen that at the poker table."

No, I did not look like the average player—i.e., I was not a paunchy middle-aged white guy. Dreads and threads. No apologies. I'm a dandy. When it came to raising the kid, my ex-wife and I split duties according to our strengths. She did morals and ethics. I did clothes. When I took this assignment I had no idea that my plumage was going to be held against me. First my deplorable lack of tournament acumen, now this.

As a woman, an "other" at this Iron John weenie roast, Coach knew what she was talking about. "I have the same situation where you look different," she said. "They're not going to give you credit, and they're going to come after you, and you have to wait for situations to take advantage of that."

So, watch out, Little Lord Fauntleroy, with your

prancing and cavorting. On to other practical matters. Have a big breakfast. She was not a germophobe, she assured me, but she advised against getting a burger or whatever delivered to the table, as people do. "If that fell on the floor, I would probably eat it. But the poker chips is filth. It's filthy." She didn't have to tell me. I end every excursion outside my front door with a Purell rubdown. Nook and cranny, baby. "That's why I enjoy a banana or Snicker's bar," Coach confided. "Because it has its own wrapper, and you just hold the wrapper."

And perhaps most important of all: Potty Rules. At break, you got hundreds of dudes stampeding to take a piss at the same time. The queues for the women's were no biggie—the one perk of low female participation—but the men's was ludicrous. Duck out during the levels to use the john, or else "you'll be spending your break time in line." Plus, I added to myself, it would give me more time to survey my anxieties between play.

I wrote it all down, feeling like a jerk. Staked to play in the Main Event, here I was picking the brain of someone so obviously in love with the game—the rushes, the science, the sheer dynamism of it—and she isn't going to be there. She'd dipped into the circuit for nine months, flown out for the WSOP, but hadn't made it into the Big Game.

Per the racial-harmony movie script, I was supposed to give something back. What kind of Magic Negro was

I? Sheesh. I had, as a child, thought Doug Henning to be a "cool dresser" and "kind of a badass," but digging an eccentric magician's clothes sense and metaphysical je ne sais quoi was not enough to make you Will Smith or Michael Clarke Duncan in an Oscar-bait film, melanin aside. I should have been delivering homilies, sucking out sickness by laying on my healing hands, helping some catatonic little white kid come out of his shell, whatever the fuck, and all I could do was take notes.

I was playing for Methy Mike and Big Mitch and the other home-game slobs, but of course I was also playing for Helen now. I recorded her wisdom and pledged to play according to the teachings of my sensei, and try not to mess it up too much.

....

"Get into your spine," Kim said. "Get into your body." I was getting into my spine, I was getting into my body. Per instructions, I imagined a string that traveled through my head into my spinal column, and that the rest of my body dangled off it: the Marionette, they called it. "I want you to feel supported, and unsupported." It was easy to relate to being a puppet, under the sway of some malevolent and capricious puppet master: This was already a close approximation of my relationship with my deity. In Kim's studio—as the fan almost covered the noise from the playground across the street and the ambulance hustling by—I pictured myself floating through the Rio Casino in Las Vegas, past the rows and rows of the barking slots and the creatures who clawed their hands through big, white chum buckets of coins, deep breath in, past the crowd huddled around the craps table as they cheered on some lucky devil's rush, deep breath out, past the cheapo blackjack tables and the high-stakes blackjack tables and the cordoned-off rooms of the super high rollers, which were always empty save for the eerily patient dealer, and into the Pavilion, the chamber as large as a football field where the tournament unfolded, the numbers and color codes hanging from the ceiling on wires, where my first seat of the tourney awaited my rebuilt posture. Shuffle up and deal.

"Did you get what you wanted out of it?" Kim asked. It was our last training session. Yes, I had. I could use this. Nowadays, whenever I watched James Bond fly across the world to Shanghai to karate chop a mad genius, I couldn't help but think, "But what about the jet lag? Isn't he pooped out from the jet lag?" Under Kim's tutelage, I felt younger, de-harrowed, as if time were reversing itself. Even my gray hair had disappeared. Or so I thought. My ex-wife and I had owned white-haired cats, and it turned out I'd only washed the remnants of their hair out of my dreadlocks.

"I bet you have a good poker face," Kim said. "You're hard to read. Most people, you can tell if they're having an easy time or if something is painful. With you, you can't really tell—"

"My blank face—"

"It's hard to tell."

There it was again. For years and years, people had told me I had a good poker face. When they heard I was going to play cards at a friend's on Friday night, or I ran into them on the subway while carrying my suitcase of monogrammed chips, which was a gift from a college buddy after I was a groomsman in his wedding, they'd say: "I bet you have a good poker face." They don't know a set of trips from a royal flush, but they know this fact. What they're really saying is: You are a soulless monster whose fright mask is incapable of capturing normal human expressions. You are a throwback to a Neanderthal state of raw, uncomplicated emotions, or a harbinger of our cold, passionless future, but either way, I don't know what's going on in your head.

Perhaps I am projecting.

Nonetheless, we have now definitely waded into the waters of training area numero three, *EXISTENTIAL*:

I can't help it if I understand that everything tends to ruin. Over our heads, Skylab is eternally falling down, I can see it all, the debris raining without cessation. I was a skinny guy, but I was morbidly obese with doom. By disposition, I was keyed into the entropic part of gambling, which says that, eventually, you will lose it all. The House always wins. Even for the most talented players, the cards fail for weeks or months or years, the beats are the baddest of the bad, you are blinded out of existence. Remember how I mentioned the blinds and how they escalate at intervals? If you don't keep ahead of them by doubling up your stack, they'll eliminate you. This is what I knew now: They are a Wave of Mutilation. You survive one wave of a Big Blind, then the half-size one of the Small Blind, diminished, and then the next wave starts gathering force down-table. I was in tune with decay, I had it down. What I needed to do was get in touch with decay's opposing force, whatever that thing is that gets us out of bed each day and keeps us a few steps ahead of the wave: the hope of some good cards next hand.

For the citizens of the Republic of Anhedonia, luck is merely the temporary state of outrunning your impending disasters. But sometimes my countrymen and I have to look beyond our native truths and pray. Even a temporary respite from the usual level of soul-snuffing drudgery is a blessing. Luck would have to do. You need skill in poker, but you also need the puppet master to be in a good mood every once in a while. I didn't have much skill, but I'd prepared the best I could. I suppose I could have run simulations of previous World Series on the holodeck, but I didn't have a holodeck, at least one I want to talk about. Luck would have to carry me where my training failed.

I packed. Arranged my affairs. Was there anyone I'd forgotten to disappoint before I took off? It'd be a while before I returned, and I didn't want to leave them hanging. On the morning of Friday, July 8, I hopped a plane to Vegas to play in the Main Event. Like one of my beautiful losers, I would step on the scale before a live studio audience and we'd all see how much bad stuff I had shed.

WRETCH LIKE ME

I pity people who've never been to Vegas. Who dismiss the city without setting foot on its carpeted sidewalks. I'll forgive the sanctimony in the question "But what do you *do* there?" The obnoxious self-regard. Sanctimony and self-regard are as American as smallpox blankets and supersize meals. As a foreigner, I make a point never to judge the cultural norms of my adopted country.

The pity remains, however. Frank Sinatra, the king of Rat Pack–era Vegas, once said, "I feel sorry for people who don't drink. When they wake up in the morning, that's as good as they're going to feel all day." The world is a disease you shake off in the desert. To delude yourself that you are a human being with thoughts and feelings, when your experience is but the shadow of truly living—it moves me to tears. Although I should note that in Anhedonian, the word *tears* means "to shrug in a distinctive 'well, what are you gonna do?' fashion," and has nothing to do with lachrymal fluids produced by glands in the eye.

I recognized myself in the town the first time I laid eyes on it, during a cross-country trip the summer after college. My friend Darren had a gig writing for *Let's Go*, the student-run series of travel guides. *Let's Go USA*, *Let's Go Europe*, *Let's Go North Korea* (they always lost a few freshmen putting that one together). The previous year his beat had been New York City. We spent the summer eating fifty-cent hot dogs at Gray's Papaya for breakfast, lunch, and dinner, and "researching" dive bars like Downtown Beirut and King Tut's Wah Wah Hut, which were beacons of pure, filthy truth in a city still years away from its Big Cleanup. This summer he was assigned the Southwest. The subways didn't run that far out, but his roommate Dan had a car, a brown '83 Toyota Tercel, and the idea was we'd hit the open road and split the writing duties and money three ways.

It was 1991. We'd just been diagnosed as "Generation X," and certainly had all the symptoms, our designs and life plans as scrawny and undeveloped as our bodies. Sure, we had dreams. Dan had escaped college with a degree in visual arts, was a cartoonist en route to becoming an animator. Darren was an anthro major who'd turned to film, fancying himself a David Lynch–style auteur in those early days of the indie art-house wave. I considered myself a writer but hadn't gotten much further than wearing black and smoking cigarettes. I wrote two five-page short stories, two five-page epics, to audition for my college's creative writing workshops, and was turned down both times. I was crushed, but in retrospect it was perfect training for being a writer. You can keep "Write What You Know"—for a true apprenticeship, internalize the world's indifference and accept rejection and failure into your very soul.

First thing, Dan hooked up our ride with new speakers. We didn't have money or prospects, but we had our priorities straight. No, I couldn't drive, those days being the template of my passengerness. That spring, on schedule, I swore I'd get my license so I could contribute my fair share, but no. Look, I know how to drive, I'm just not legal. I took driver's ed, but never got around to taking the road test. Never mind that I passed the class on false pretenses. I shot up half a foot junior year and had weird growing pains, like an excruciating stinging in my neck if I turned my head too fast. So every time the instructor led me into busy Broadway traffic, or told me to merge onto the West Side Highway, I faked it. I'd turn my head a little to simulate checking my blind spot and hope for the best. Everyone has blind spots. The magnitude of my self-sabotage was such that I willfully ignored all of mine. If you don't look, you can pretend nothing is gaining on you.

I promised to make it up to Dan and Darren by being

a Faithful Navigator, wrestling with the Rand McNally and feeding the cassette deck with dub. Dub, Lee "Scratch" Perry, deep deep cuts off side six of *Sandinista!*—let these be indicators of the stoner underpinnings of our trip out West. As if our eccentric route were not enough. From New York down to Lancaster, Pennsylvania, to visit a college pal. He took me to my first mall. Even then, I had a weakness for those prefab palaces. "I asked Andy why there were no security guards around," I wrote in my notebook. "He told me I had a New Yorker's mentality."

Then hundreds of miles up to Chicago for a disappointing pilgrimage too complicated and inane to detail here. We bought two tiny replicas of the Sears Tower as consolation. Veered south, taking in the territory, cooking up plots. Inspiration: "discussing the plot of the movie Darren wants to write, about 7-Elevens that land in cornfields." Down to New Orleans, where we slept in a frat house on mattresses still moldy and damp from the spring flood. One of Darren's childhood friends belonged to the frat. His brothers wanted to know why he was "bringing niggers and Jews" into their chill-space. We sure were seeing a lot of America on this trip.

Then west to tackle our *Let's Go* assignment proper. Bull's horns and turquoise rocks. We wrote up the Grand Canyon, which almost rivaled our Great Trouble Ditch back home, where on the vernal equinox we burn offerings to Saint Gus, who drove the smiles out of Anhedonia with nothing more than an electric zither and a list of proof. Hit Lake Mead, which also summoned pleasant memories of another homeland monument, the Puddle of Sorrows, where we held Senior Prom.

Decided to keep driving so we could spend the night in Las Vegas, the camping thing not really taking. ("Hours of agony. Impossible to sleep. Bugs. A consistent feeling of itchiness.") Miles and miles of black hills and winding roads and then at one crest it manifested, this smart white jellyfish flopping on the desert floor. We suited up in a cheap motel downtown. Anticipating all the sweaty, laundryless days and nights we'd spend in the Tercel, we'd hit Domsey's, the famous Brooklyn thrift store, before we left NYC. We required proper gear for our Vegas debut. Dead men's spats, ill-fitting acrylic slacks, and blazers with stiff fibers sticking out of the joints and seams. Roll up the sleeves of the sports jacket to find the brown stains from the previous owner's track marks. We looked great.

The whole trip out I'd maintained that I wasn't going to gamble. Gambling was a weakness of the ignorant masses, the suckers inhabiting the Great American Middle we'd just driven through. I was an intellectual, see, could quote Beckett on the topic of the abyss, had a college degree and everything. Humming a few bars of the Slacker National Anthem here. I had a nickel in my pocket, though. I can't remember the name of our hotel, the place is long demolished to make room for the Fremont Street Experience. It wasn't a proper casino, just a grim box with rooms upstairs, but the first floor had rows of low-stakes gambling apparatus to keep the reception desk company. On our way to check-in, we passed the geriatric zombies in tracksuits installed at the slots, empty coin buckets overturned on their oxygen tanks. These gray-skinned doomed tugged on the levers, blinked, tugged again. Blink. Tug. Blink.

Grisly. But I had a nickel. We were about to get our first glimpse of the hurly-burly of downtown Vegas. To stroll past Binion's Horseshoe, in fact, where the twenty-second World Series of Poker had just wrapped up. Two hundred and fifteen people strong. The winner, Brad Daugherty, got a million bucks. Not that I knew that then. I was contemplating the nickel in my hand. Before we pushed open the glass doors, what the heck, I dropped it into a one-armed bandit and won two dollars.

In a dank utility room deep in the subbasements of my personality, a little man wiped his hands on his overalls and pulled the switch: *More.* Remembering it now, I hear a sizzling sound, like meat being thrown into a hot skillet. I didn't do risk, generally. So I thought. But I see now I'd been testing the House Rules the last few years. I'd always been a goody-goody. Study hard, obey your parents, hut-hut-hut through the training exercises of Decent Society. Then in college, now that no one was around, I started to push the boundaries, a little more each semester. I was an empty seat in lecture halls, slept late in a depressive funk, handed in term papers later and later to see how much I could get away with before the House swatted me down.

Push it some more. We go to casinos to tell the everyday world that we will not submit. There are rules and codes and institutions, yes, but for a few hours in this temple of pure chaos, of random cards and inscrutable dice, we are in control of our fates. My little gambles were a way of pretending that no one was the boss of me. I didn't have time for driving lessons before our trip because I was too busy cramming a semester of work into exam period. It had been touch and go whether I'd graduate, as I'd barely shown up for my final semester's Religion course. The last thing I wanted to hear about was some sucker notion of the Divine. There's a man in the sky who watches over everything you do, as all-seeing as the thousands of security cameras embedded in casino ceilings. So what? Nothing escapes his attention, and nothing will move him to intervene.

After a few phone calls, the administration released me into the world with a D-minus. What was it to them? My passive-aggressive rebellion against the system was meaningless. The House doesn't care if you piss away your chances, are draining Loretta's college fund, letting the plumber's invoice slide until next month. Ruin yourself. The cameras above record it all, but you're just another sap passing in the night.

The nickels poured into the basin, sweet music. If it worked once, it will work again.

We hit the street.

Before we left town, we bought dozens of tiny plastic slot machines from a trinket shop. Pink, red, lime green. They joined the Museum of Where We'd Been. Everybody's a walking Museum of Where They've Been, but we decided to make it literal. We had serious epoxy. Each place we stopped, we picked up souvenirs and glued them to the hood of our jalopy. Two Sears Towers sticking up over the engine, a row of small turquoise stones on the roof just above the windshield, toy buffalo stampeding across the great brown plain over the engine. Bull's horns from Arizona, in case we needed to gore someone at ramming speed, you never know, and four refrigerator magnets with Elvis's face on the front grille, to repel ghosts. We dotted the hood with glue and stuck the slot machines on, to show everyone where we'd been, the polyethylene totems marking us as goofball heathens.

Weeks later, we were in Berkeley, sleeping on a friend's floor. The friend was cat-sitting for a drug dealer, weed mostly. I didn't approve of the drug dealer's lifestyle choices—for vacation, he went camping. We wrote up our time in the land of Circus Circus and El Cortez, the cheap steaks and watered-down drinks. *Let's Go*'s previ-

ous correspondent had been a prissy little shit, filling his/
her copy with snobby asides. "But what do you *do* there?"
He/she wrote:

> *Forget Hollywood images of Las Vegas glamour, the city
> at base is nothing but a desert Disneyland. As a small,
> small world of mild, middle-aged debauchery, Vegas
> simply replaces Minnie and Mickey with overbright,
> neon marquees, monolithic hotel/casinos, besequinned
> Ziegfeldesque entertainers, quickly marrying them in
> rococo wedding chapels.*

Percy, where are my smelling salts? What's wrong
with Disneyland? It brings joy to millions and tutors
children about the corporate, overbranded world they've
been born into. "It's a Small World" is a delightful ditty,
an ode to that quality of everyday existence by which the
soul is crushed, diminished, *made entirely small*. No need
to denigrate it. Better to worry about the lack of a clear
antecedent for *them* in that last sentence. I would protect
Vegas. How about:

> *The magic formula of mild, middle-aged debauchery—
> offer everything but the gambling cheaply, and if you
> gild it, they will come—was hit upon by Bugsy Siegel in
> the 1940s. Das Kapital is worshipped here, and sacrifices
> from all major credit cards are accepted.*

Much more upbeat, although I apologize if some readers were tricked into thinking the city is dedicated to Karl Marx's book. I think we were just trying to get fancy with "Capital."

Some of the classic joints we wrote about are gone now, and we captured a time before Las Vegas made a science of demography, but most of the basic observations in our *Let's Go* entry remain solid. In between games of Risk (board-game version), we cut up the previous year's text, discarded what we disliked, and glued (more glue) what remained onto white paper alongside our revisions and additions. "But remember that casinos function on the basis of most tourists leaving considerably closer to the poverty line than when they arrived; don't bring more than you're prepared to lose cheerfully" became "But always remember: *in the long run, chances are you're going to lose money.* Don't bring more than you're prepared to lose cheerfully." No, casinos are not out to destroy you. The destroyed do not return to redeem reward-card perks and lose more money. No one forces doom upon you, folks. You need to seek it out.

We kept "Drinks in most casinos cost 75¢–$1, free to those who look like they're playing," but added "Look like you're gambling; acting skills will stretch your wallet, but don't forget to tip that cocktail waitress in the interesting get-up." Out with the general tsk-tsking and upper-middle-class disdain, and in with "For best results, put on your favorite loud outfit, bust out the cigar and pinkie rings, and begin." You have been granted a few days' reprieve from who you are. Celebrate the gift of a place that allows you to be someone else for a time.

I don't know who wrote that the Excalibur "has a medieval theme that will make you nostalgic for the Black Plague," but it wasn't me. Pretty sure.

California. Pretentious pseudo-intellectual or no, I was not immune to the Western dream of reinvention. All that cultural programming about the freedom of the frontier had stuck, even if I pictured myself more in the *Day of the Locust* version. The entire trip I thought I was going to stay in California. I had nothing to go back to. No job. No bed but my parents' couch. No nice girlfriend waiting for me, or even a mean one. We smoked weed, played Risk, time passed. One day we got word there was going to be a riot in People's Park, at 1:00 p.m. sharp. They scheduled riots there. It gave order to our lives.

We dropped one by one. Darren wigged out and caught a plane home. He still had his childhood room. Dan was going to drive back east in August, maybe get a Eurail pass that autumn and check out some fucking castles or whatever. I was out of money when Dan set off, and I asked if he had any room in the car, as the guy we'd been crashing with, the cat-sitter, was bailing out of California, too, and bringing all his stuff. After all, I was a good navigator. As luck would have it, they intended to stop off in Vegas on the way back.

No one laid a hand on the Museum when we were on the road. Odd, moonfaced kids—a motel owner's brood—gawked at them when we stopped at night but dared not touch. A cop pulled us over for speeding in Massachusetts the last day of our return trip. "What's all this?" We shrugged. What to say? He wrote us a ticket. The Museum lasted a few days in Cambridge before teenagers or disaffected housewives or whoever stripped everything. We'd made it home, and the spell had worn off.

We grew up. Our generational symptoms faded bit by bit. I got a job working for the book section of a newspaper. We ran fiction sometimes, mixed in with reviews. When the writing teacher who'd rejected my work in college submitted a story, I passed on it. Not out of revenge, it just wasn't up to snuff. As in cards, it was business, not personal. I badgered one editor for an assignment, that assignment led to another, and somehow I was paying my bills freelancing. Played poker at Dan's house every Sunday for a couple of years, and one day we picked up Hold'em. Dan got into computers and founded a visual-effects company, rendering CGI for movies such as *Requiem for a Dream* and *Black Swan*, which Darren directed. We waited for cards, and then we played them.

And here I was, writing about Vegas again.

. . . .

"This wasn't here the last time I came," I said.

"Yes, and look at it," Jon said. "It is shit."

My first night in town. Tumbling into the new City-Center array, a virtual money sink, a highly evolved specimen of the Leisure Industrial Complex that seemed almost self-aware once you entered its nimbus, bristling with enchantments 24/7.

"Wow," I said. The highway lifted and aimed us into the CityCenter's black, glass heart. The dark buildings of the complex surrounded us, sheer residential towers and curvilinear hotels. Pure fury made concrete, shot through with rebar.

It was Jon's car. He was the first person to take me to a casino, one of the AC Trumps, back in '96. My college roommate, currently a kind of nightlife broker in Vegas, managing a stable of video DJs, and flitting around the city at night as "Director of Programming" for hot spots that sounded like an erotic tasting menu: Blush, Surrender, Encore. Showing me around and explaining the rules once more.

Jon worked under the handle "Shecky Green," the latest incarnation of his ongoing character, Mr. Entertainment. Mr. Entertainment stepped onstage during Jon's teens. After his stint as one half of white rap duo B.M.O.C., he launched the legendary music mag *The Source* ("The Magazine of Hip-Hop Music, Culture & Politics") in his dorm room. I lived with him the following year. Long before I tangled with collection agencies, rooming with Shecky introduced me to answering-machine dread. You never knew when you might be pummeled by a string of cussing by Luther Campbell, frustrated over a mixed review of "We Want Some Pussy," or his inability to think up interesting choruses.

After cashing out of *The Source*, Shecky cast himself in a series of entrepreneurial roles—publisher of a Gen-X *Playboy*, manager of a record label—before making bank with his bestselling *Hip Hop Honeys* DVDs, a single-minded hopscotch around the world in search of booty-enabled beauties: *Hip Hop Honeys: Brazil Boom Boom*, *Hip Hop Honeys: Blazin' Asians. Hip Hop Honeys: Las Vegas*, natch. He even ventured in front of the camera as the on-air commentator for a late-night poker show called *Hip Hop Hold'em*, which ran for a while in 2006 when all sorts of poker shows weaseled themselves into America's programming grids. Method Man and Ed Lover playing loose, quite a sight, and Shecky spieling on the sidelines. "The 8 has arrived, and Biz Markie makes a straight!" No matter the arena, nobody beats the Biz.

Shecky took me along as he made his nightly rounds of restaurants and clubs. First up: CityCenter. Despite its $9 billion price tag and 1.5 million square feet of space, the CityCenter ("Capital of the New World") had not turned out to be the flaneur-friendly wonderland prom-ised in the brochures. Shecky lived in one of the residential towers. I put my nose to the window: pretty tony from the outside. The recession derailed things, though. Busto sales, cascading foreclosures, squatters taking over the empty units. Gruesome machete fights in the laundry rooms over who's next up on the driers, just like Brooklyn.

"They said it would look like Central Park," Shecky said. "Look, those are the trees." He gestured toward a lonesome half dozen slouching out of the cement. I didn't see any street retail on our approach, no inviting boulevards, no place to wander except into the entrances of the casinos. But what casinos! They were the magnificent embodiment of scientifically derived LIC principles: gargantuan in scale, single-minded in execution. A pure expression of consumer will. The old days were gone, like the Dunes, the Sands, all the Rat Pack warrens imploded by dynamite charges, dust. In their places these beautiful monsters emerged from the rubble: the Bellagio, the Venetian.

And the Cosmopolitan. Shecky led me there, into this ebony monolith whose name was bolted in huge letters across the top floor, more fitting for a corporate headquarters than a hotel. I appreciated the honesty. The developers had hoped for a nice crop of condos, but after the downturn the soil was exhausted. Deutsche Bank took over, apartments became hotel rooms, and the first floor a hypermodern casino. In the Vegas war of gambling versus places for people to live, the money wins out, I imagine.

◆

Windows were scarce, per standard casino style, the mammoth footprint of the building creating the illusion of a banquet room without walls. All you can eat—this is the Land of Fabled Buffets, after all—you walked on and on, never satiated. Trudging through the main floor of the Cosmo on a weekend night, you were one of tens of thousands of hungry souls. Addled. Cortexes popping. Prey to sundry appetites. What's next? Where's next? One of your party was sucked into an eddy of diversion over there and had to be rescued by texted coordinates: Let's reconnoiter over by the Pai Gow or the chanteuse who's just mounted the platform by the crystal stairs. Micro-entertainments popped up here and there like brief sun-showers, suddenly somebody's singing on a tiny stage for a couple of old standards, and then they split. Poof, into nightlife vapor.

The Cosmopolitan's nightclub was called Marquee, up on the terrace. It was quite splendid. Hotel clubs like Marquee had a dependable schedule of colada-soaked pool parties during the day, followed by quiet time for disco naps and "What's up? Oh, nothing" calls home at dusk, and then another hard skid of partying until dawn. I wanted to stay, I wanted to live there. I'd scoop the hair-balls and condoms from the drains in the pool, whatever. Shecky did business. At every new venue he'd say, "I have to talk to this guy for a minute," yelling so I could hear him above the electro music, and then confer with his opposite number at this establishment. Nodding, yes, yes.

Mr. Entertainment had found a home. Vegas hadn't changed him—he had always been Vegas, now he was more so. Why shouldn't an enterprising white guy from Philadelphia create a landmark rap magazine, assemble an empire of honeys, ringmaster the billion-dollar nightlife of a hungry city? Follow his dream. Not the American dream but the desert dream of finding your oasis in the wasteland. To everyone else it is a mirage, a trick of the eyes in the infernal heat. Until you lead them to it, and they taste the waters for themselves.

These were his people, dancing. Seventy-two hours in another city, to try on a new self, this table image. Since the disco was grafted onto a residential structure, access came by way of unadorned fire stairwells, which at peak traffic were inundated with wobbly bachelorettes on stilettos, Jager-blind groomsmen, and leather-skinned jet-setters creaking in crisp designer duds who passed each other up and down the stairs with a delirious urgency. A scene from the inferior American remake of *The Discreet Charm of the Bourgeoisie*, or lost footage from *The Towering Inferno*. I still recognized myself here. Monster places for monster people. Like I said, I wanted to move in.

....

Speaking of Brazil. The Rio had been the home of the WSOP the past couple of years. Like a teenager rolling her eyes at her parents' cornpone ways, the place rejected the architectural kitsch of old-school Vegas—the miniature cityscape of New York–New York, the Paris's Eiffel Tower replication—to run the streets with the slab architecture of the new megacasinos. But really, what could the Rio have been shaped like? A twenty-story toucan? I'm sure they thought about it.

The lightly enforced Brazilian theme disappeared altogether once you got to the convention hall, where the World Series had been chugging along for six weeks with a host of lower-stakes Hold'em events, Seven Card Razz, and the like. The declivity of the Hall of Legends was festooned with huge banners featuring the blown-up faces of game greats—devilish Scotty Nguyen, a grim-looking Erick Lindgren, last year's champ Jonathan Duhamel. Then it was into the rotunda, where you could buy snacks, beef jerky, and WSOP merch. Smack in the middle of the rotunda was a WSOP display, featuring a TV monitor that replayed last year's Final Table on a loop day and night. When I tried to register the morning of my start, at 6:00 a.m. (I hadn't been sleeping well, I had been sleeping quite poorly), the announcer's voice echoed in the empty halls. Nobody there at that hour. Everybody'd seen it already anyway.

The afternoon of my arrival, the hallways brimmed

with desperados, the Pavilion and Amazon Rooms awhir. I stepped into the Pavilion. The first thing I noticed—this was before the size of the room assaulted my brain—was the crickets. The chips clicked and clicked, thousands of players fiddled with their chips, stacking them, tossing them into the pot, scooping them up, dealers counting off All Ins, click click click. Cricket symphony.

There were more than two hundred tables, ten-seated, which meant they could shoehorn in a lot of runners. It was Day 1B, and the Main Event was under way in the Green Section, the Black Section, etc., while in one corner players ground through satellite games, still hoping to win a seat in the World Series. The buy-in was ten grand, but pay five-hundred-something bucks in a satellite, make it into the top of the field, and you won a ticket to the Big Game. So while Main Event players were washing out just beyond the velvet rope, these bruisers slugged it out for the opportunity. Some of them had been here for weeks. The clock was ticking. If they got bounced, there was time to enter another one, one more last chance. You can play as many as you like, satellite after satellite. Same principle as slot machines, just a lot slower.

The Amazon Room was smaller, around the corner past the vendors peddling poker primers and arcane table spectacles ("Hide Your Eyes"), the registration areas, and the Poker Kitchen, where you could grab a quick sub or a salad. I assume the name of the joint depended on the current occupants of the convention hall. "Hot Grub" for the entomologists' annual get-together, and something appropriately farm-to-autopsy table for the forensic scientists.

The Amazon was where the ESPN cameras roosted. The network's WSOP programming crept up every year to feed the aficionados. They were spitting out unprecedented coverage this year, on cable and multiple internet streams, so the room was exuberantly branded by the sports channel and the World Series's main sponsor, Jack Link's Beef Jerky. What, you don't like beef jerky? You got your Peppered Beef Jerky, Teriyaki Beef Jerky, it's a convenient source of protein in an easy-seal pouch. Young correspondents from the trades—*Bluff Magazine* and *Card Player*—scooted between the tables, here's a status report on the big guns, can I snap a pic for the liveblog, something for the fans back home? Portly security guards shuffled between the velvet ropes. You'd almost think there was real money on the felt.

....

TV cameras snipered down on the two Feature Tables, which were situated apart from the regular sections, percolating under garish blue and crimson lights. On Day 1C Brad Garrett from *Everybody Loves Raymond* did his time at one. He was known for his poker acumen, striking a menacing glare from the cover of *Bluff*, which was blown up and perched on easels throughout the halls. Headline news: "Black Friday: The D.O.J. Shuts Down the Big 3," referring to the online sites Full Tilt Poker, Absolute Poker, and PokerStars. Brad and his TV brother, Ray Romano, yukked it up while playing, their TV bond no act and still going strong these long years into undead syndication. We should be so lucky.

Celebrities of various wattage. Jason Alexander, staked by PokerStars, who were keeping up a brave front despite the Feds. Paul Pierce of the Celtics. The rapper Nelly, or so I was told, and Shannon Elizabeth, who was a celebrity, or so I was told. The poker luminaries in their firmament, the guys who wrote the books and cranked out the instructional videos, recognizable from the poker TV shows you may have watched at home or endured in a hotel bar. They were being overthrown, these kings. Was this the Main Event or the Deadliest Game? Doyle Brunson, a.k.a. Texas Dolly (after his collection of vintage Barbies, most of them still in the original packaging), da Godfather, went out two hours into Day 1A. Greg Raymer and Jerry Yang, two former world champions, hit the rails, and Matt Affleck, too. What are you going to do?

Michael "The Grinder" Mizrachi, whose madcappery had livened last year's TV coverage, was strafed to bits while crawling on his knees and elbows toward a straight draw. His farewell *Saving Private Ryan* tweet

♦

to his three brothers, who also played: "Officially out of the Main Event!! Sour start to the day!! Good Lucky my brothers!! Sorry left you guys behind!!" If they were going out, what chance a wretch like me? About 1,400 runners atomized by the time I played on Day 1D.

I railed for two days, watching, trying to get accustomed to the ebb and flow of the place. Listening to the crickets.

....

Reward cards and rejuvenating foot massages. Look for sawdust on the floors, and you will not find it. We were not at Binion's Horseshoe, home of the inaugural World Series. Downtown Vegas, 1970, before TV rights, trademarked merch, bleached teeth. Only forty-odd years ago, but let's picture it in sepia, for kicks. There were seven bare-knuckle entrants, cronies of casino owner Benny Binion, and no official prize money. The players voted on the winner, Johnny Moss, who received an engraved silver cup. This year there were 6,856 entrants, and the top 10 percent got paid off, with the champion paying taxes on $8,715,638 in winnings.

Al Alvarez immortalized the early days of the spectacle in *The Biggest Game in Town*. That book, and James McManus's *Positively Fifth Street: Murderers, Cheetahs, and Binion's World Series of Poker*, are lively, bravura accounts of the Main Event before Chris Moneymaker's inspirational fable destroyed the old paradigm. Alvarez—a poet, editor, and essayist—attended the 1981 festivities, which had ticked up to a field of seventy-three warriors. The cowboys still reigned, charging through the sagebrush in a romantic fable of colorful personalities, savage talent, once-in-a-lifetime convergences. "Romance," Alvarez writes, "because that's how the poker pros saw themselves: as the last of the gunslingers, ready to showdown with any stranger who dared to take them on." Pew pew.

Call me a dandy, sure, but Alvarez's outlaws with their "Stetsons, embroidered shirts, and bolo ties" were no slackers in the sartorial department. Yosemite Sam and his rootin'-tootin' glamour are deep in the chromosomes of the game, gunfight lingo permeating the vernacular. Chips are *ammo*, *bullets* a pair of Aces. A *shootout* is a tourney where you advance only when everyone else at your table is exterminated, and in a *bounty* you grabbed bonuses for cutting down certain players. Polish the chaps and saddle up, boys and girls.

Alvarez was an Englishman, a foreigner like me, chatting up poker legends like Johnny Moss and Doyle Brunson, as well as pseudonymous high rollers whose lunatic attitudes toward money were queasy evidence of the gambler mentality. Chapter by chapter, we traversed the gangplank to the original Showboat: "It was as if the old riverboat cardsharps had never been quite exorcised and now they were back again . . . reincarnated as gnarled, relentless good ol' boys who knew how to turn on the charm but never gave a sucker an even break."

The 1981 game was still run by the Binion family. A closed fraternity of hard-bitten pros and the well-heeled fish foolish enough to tangle with them. Before TV cameras and poker memoirs, *The Biggest Game in Town* was as close as most regular enthusiasts were ever going to come to the action. Lucky them: Alvarez's portraiture was warmhearted and wry, the enthusiasm of a good pal who saves you a primo spot at the rail. He was a less unctuous version of Saul Rubinek in *Unforgiven*, the penny-dreadful scribe chronicling the lethal day-to-day of Little Bill and the Duck of Death, setting down high-noon showdowns for the audience safe at home, far from the frontier.

Like many humans, writers need money for food and travel. *The New Yorker* underwrote Alvarez's trip to Vegas. McManus traveled out on *Harper's* dime to chronicle the 2000 Main Event and the death of Ted Binion, son of Benny, who'd taken over operations at the Horseshoe. *Positively Fifth Street* toggled between McManus's coverage of the Binion murder trial (narcotics, desert gangsters, the attendant autopsies), his tentative dips into Vegas strip-club culture (the Cheetahs of the subtitle), and his miraculous Main Event adventure.

McManus was a poet and fiction writer, but also an amateur poker player. Hells yeah, he was going to play a little while out West. Internet gaming was just a sparkle of code in some programmer's eye, so McManus crammed the books (as you do) and pointed and clicked through rudimentary computer games, whose crappy graphics I can only imagine. Shudder. Once he arrived, he parleyed a $200 satellite into a seat at the Main Event. His passage was not without hardship (it's stressful, dude) but the improbably badass conclusion was exhilarating—the Final Table, where he placed third and raked in almost a quarter of a million dollars. Holy megillah!

When the book version of his underdog story was published in 2003, it helped popularize the myth of the Rise of the Amateur. Chris Moneymaker's Main Event coup that year, and the internet gaming that made it possible, detonated the World Series as if it were some faded Sinatra hangout hogging development space on the Strip. Moneymaker, a humble accountant, earned a trip to Vegas after wiring forty bucks for an online satellite. Here's to new blood: He ended up winning the whole shebang, 2.5 million bucks, besting poker maestros and star-crossed chumps, sidestepping bad fortune all the while.

Quake and tremble before the terrible power of the "Moneymaker Effect." The guys at home—Miller Lite wisping out of their pores and into the upholstery of their fave recliners, the latest arguments with the wife and the most recent workplace humiliations buzzing in their brains—said to themselves: "I can do that. I'm the best player in my weekly game, everyone says so." The Moneymaker mythology was a version of a core gambling fantasy: I am different from those losers I see on the street every day, this time I will prove it has not been all for naught. I am a winner.

Various forces had intersected. In 1998, *Rounders* triggered Hold'em fever among the kids. They start playing when they're sixteen, brains aswim with visions of Hollywood glory and Gretchen Mol's boobs, and then nascent internet sites give them a chance to play tournaments night and day, fueled by microwave burritos and Red Bull. TV shows like *World Poker Tour*, which debuted in 2003, insert them elbow to elbow with poker heavyweights in all their kooky glory. The camera as railbird, sweating foul-mouthed Scotty Nguyen, cranky Phil Hellmuth. Shoot, this is a racket where severe personality deficits aren't a hindrance for once. And might even help. If you're half dead inside, for example.

The books, the divine primers—Harrington's trilogy, and the thousand-plus pages of Brunson's *Super System*—delivered Prometheus's fire to the hoodied cavemen. When Moneymaker, account holder at PokerStars.com, *one of them*, wins his bracelet, we have entered a new age, when knuckle-dragging wretches can grab a seat at the table. In McManus's 2000 game the field was 512. In Moneymaker's game, 839. The next year, attendance tripled to 2,500 hopefuls. By 2006, 8,000 players showed up at the

Rio—sharps, internet homunculi, Sarasota dentists, and hedge-fund dinks with $10K in disposable cash. America was in a cash bubble, and so was organized poker.

The Binion family sold off the casino and Harrah's Entertainment picked up the rights to the WSOP in 2004. It's big biz, like everything else in town. Walking the Rio floors, the machine hums, you can barely hear it. There is no such thing as a seedy underbelly when everybody's on their back, airing out their bits. You smile indulgently at the minor vulgarities described by Alvarez—hookers making propositions in elevators, the imbecilic stage shows—as years of viral YouTube atrocities, C-listers' sex tapes, and a million texted nudie shots have collapsed the travel time to the desert. Like Shecky Green, we are all a bit Vegas now, more comfortable exposing ourselves in all our weaknesses and appetites. Goodbye cowboy, hello middle-class schlub.

McManus covered a murder trial, the specters of drugs and organized crime circling his stories of the Main Event like tourists around the crab-claw tray at an all-you-can-eat. That kind of trouble, real trouble, permanent trouble, puts a dent in visitor-retention stats. The only crimes I witnessed during my stay this time were some ill-considered shirts and multiple counts of misdemeanor hairdos.

....

♦

McManus's deep run in the Main Event not only made him the Man among amateur players but likened him unto a god to amateur player-scribblers. Shoot, he earned his way into his seat. I had my entrance fee handed to me. (Assuming it showed up. We'll get to that.) The shame.

I didn't have illusions about being one of the November Nine. We live in an age in which sitcoms outnumber miracles, and perhaps that is what we deserve. The amateurs were thumping the fabled cowboys these days, but I was an amateur's amateur. I didn't want to go out first, and I wanted to make it to Day 3 at least. Day 3 had the sheen of respectability. I would not bring dishonor to my house—my friends, family, and poker game back home. To Coach. Day 3, then take it from there.

Despite my persistent terrors about being the first one to wash out, there were four starting days to the Main Event, so the first player flamed out while I was still brooding in my Brooklyn hermit shack. Twenty minutes into Day 1A, his KKs got smithereened by Aces. Aces, Aces. He stumbled out of the hall, ducking the media, this nameless, hapless schmuck, and into the neon desert-within-a-desert that is Las Vegas. Where presumably he lost some more money.

On the bright side, that didn't mean I couldn't be the first player to wash out on my starting day.

With less than twenty-four hours to go, I made another trip to registration. I'd tried to snag my table draw earlier, but they couldn't find my check. As a writer, I was used to this. The silver-haired lady in the Cage remembered me from before and was quite helpful despite the lack of news.

"You're wearing your hair down," she said.

I like to mix it up. "Yeah. What do you think?"

"If you want to look like a badass, wear it back."

"Okay, then."

If the check didn't appear, I was fucked. I was having trouble keeping track of affronts to my psyche, but I was used to that, too. I pinballed between the ballrooms, Amazon to Brasilia, Brasilia to Pavilion, Pavilion to Amazon. Mapping the castle, the system of unmarked doors, secret passageways. This one shoots me to the terrace where I can sweat out toxins in the brutal sun, that one is a wormhole to the Poker Kitchen and its Have-It-Your-Way Wraps. And this exit is most important: for here be the johns.

After six weeks, the run-up tourneys were finished. No helter-skelter sprinting from room to room to scoop up Player of the Year points. Can anyone catch up to Ben Lamb, this year's leader? So young, Ben Lamb, such healthy skin, such psycho-killer eyes. Stray cats disappear in his hometown. Pass Lamb, bounce back after What Happened in Prague, that Cold Deck in Melbourne. The names like cities in spy novels where bad shit went down, it was Ivan's trap all along, no need to elaborate.

Whatever 2-7 Triple Draw Lowball (Limit) is, it's history, cashes added to a player's lifetime winnings on the online ledgers. The three-day Seven Card Razz, with its $2,500 buy-in. And also the niche events, such as the Casino Employees game (congrats, Sean Drake!), the Seniors event (fifty-plus only, please), and the Ladies No-Limit Championship (Marsha Wolak, represent!). The specialty events were supposed to give subcommunities a time to shine, but it didn't always work out. Last year, some bros dressed in drag and crashed the ladies' event to protest "gender discrimination." Rhinestone buckles, fringed vests, camisoles. Poker dudes: any excuse to wear something a little fancy.

The bracelets, for example, were snazzy as hell. Every sport has their trophy. What you get when you win. Stanley Cup. Super Bowl Ring. Here it's bracelets. Fifty-seven of them handed out so far this year, sparkly numbers, with fifty-two diamonds embedded in buttery white-and-yellow gold. Walk up to the 7-Eleven counter to pay for your Snapple and pork rinds, they'll know you're a man of substance, maybe throw in some scratchers, gratis. I'm reminded of the Republic of Anhedonia's Medal of Honor, the Pouch of Sighs. It's a little sack of oiled leather, stuffed with twenty-five captured sighs, that hangs around your neck on a silk lanyard. They come up on eBay from time to time, if you're interested.

The final remaining bracelet was the Big One.

Also starting on Day 1D was Matt Matros, whom I'd met eight years ago, when he was in the MFA program at Sarah Lawrence. He supported himself on poker through grad school, carving out fiction during the day and wagering at night. His book *The Making of a Poker Player: How an Ivy League Math Geek Learned to Play Championship Poker* detailed his trip to glory.

We'd only talked briefly, but Matt reached out to me when I was Rio-bound and offered to give me some tips. You may wonder why I kept meeting writers on my journey, but my social circle is quite small these days. "Why are there so many crackheads in this crackhouse?" the crackhead asked. People like that are the only people here.

Not many people know that Anhedonians invented brunch. It makes sense now that you think about it, right? Because brunch is horrible. A weekend midday food engagement was a sacrament to my kind and made me feel at home in this alien place, even if it was "ethnic food" at an establishment called the All-American Bar and Grille. It was located in a Rio eddy, where the convention hall joined the raging waters of the casino.

Old hands at the WSOP avoided the place, Matt informed me. "We're on such an absurd schedule out here," he said. "Half the tournaments start at 5:00 p.m., and they go til 3:00 in the morning and then they start the next day at 3:00 p.m." It messes with the digestion. "There's basically two thousand people all trying to eat in these restaurants and they don't hold two thousand people. So we get out of here, clear our heads, have a meal someplace we like. Nothing too heavy."

Talk about proper nutrition, and I know you're a veteran. I opened my marble notebook after apologizing for its cover, which the kid had decorated with bright-colored stickers and Cray-Pas during an impromptu "crafts project." Did McManus write in gaily colored notebooks? Hells no. But the red, yellow, and blue dots were a constellation to steer by. I was far from home, but I'd find my way back to the kid.

The last two WSOPs had been good to Matt. The previous year, he'd won the $1,500 Limit Hold'em bracelet, and in the run-up to this year's Main Event, he'd bagged the $2,500 Mixed Hold'em event ("Mixed" means alternating between Limit and No Limit, switching your brain back and forth). He pocketed $300,000 and was my Rio John McClane, creeping barefoot over glass with a machine gun, ho-ho-ho.

Not that you'd know it from Matt's low-key demeanor. This is how I judge character: If you were a stranger, would I ask you to watch my bag while I hit the coffee-shop bathroom? Not that anyone would want to steal what's in there. Breath mints. Misery beads. The matted, moth-eaten arm of a teddy bear, the final remains of my childhood companion Emilio Pepper, who taught me about love and loss. Nonetheless. I trusted Matt.

Underneath the wash of his brown hair, behind his rectangular glasses, his eyes give no indication of the multifarious calculations zipping 'round his brain. Matt had a sideline in poker coaching, which perhaps reinforced his patience with morons like me, but doubtless his composure had been perfected by years at the table. Everybody tilts, but he who tilts less, tilts best.

We chowed down. He dispensed betting tips, urged me to widen my range of starting hands, and swatted down my flurry of ignorant questions without a hint of exasperation. Like when I asked about his tribe, the Math Players.

"What's a Math Player? Just like knowing the odds and—"

"No."

"Okay."

"So when I say a Math Player, I mean . . ." The Math Players took their cues from game theory, in search of the Platonic way to play each hand. They availed themselves of the road gambler's arsenal of exploitation—bluffing, decoding tells, exploiting weak players' mistakes—when it was easy, but their holy grail was optimum play.

Exploitive play asked, How can I take advantage of this situation? The optimum play of Math Players inquires, What is the correct play for this situation? Super-aggressive chest-thumping before the flop, like sociopathic raising and re-raising when all you have is

9-3 offsuit, will fatten your stack as long as you can scare people off. But eventually exploitative players will have to duel through the Flop, the Turn, and the River, and they'll need a deeper tool kit. The Math Players insist that over time, sticking to a solid core strategy will maximize profits.

"It's not just about calculating your chances of winning," Matt told *Card Player*, "it's about calculating the correct play based on what my opponent's range of hands is, what he will do with those range of hands, how can I maximize the amount of chips I will make based on how he's gonna play. And it's very complicated." Reason trumps intuition, that staple of Hollywood poker.

It was working out so far. Matt's poker evolution tracked with many players his age, capturing Hold'em's trajectory from niche variation to its current Rio-size madness. Preflop: He started playing at fifteen with his friends out on Long Island. He wanted to rebel, but driving doughnuts on the mean bio teacher's lawn wasn't his style. "An all-night poker game," he wrote in his book, "seemed just illicit and interesting enough to be acceptable." He played in his first casino at eighteen, courtesy of a family trip to Arizona, pocketing $500 from the slots. The gateway slots, I tells ya, they change a person.

The Flop: Three years later, *Rounders* was a vista of the exotic world of Hold'em. Underground card dens, Russian mobsters, and a hero who abandons the straight life to play in the World Series of Poker. That could be you up there. Matt's dad gave him and his friends a three-page pamphlet of basic Hold'em strategy. Like many card-crazy kids his age, Matt dove into live tournaments, enrolled in night classes via the new technology. Computer programs such as the World Series of Poker Deluxe Casino Pack simulated a complete Vegas jaunt, from wheels down at McCarran International Airport to a virtual Binion's. The game even included a Gambler's Book Shop, where scholars could peruse digital excerpts from Brunson's *Super System*. Then came the poker classics on old-fashioned paper, like Sklansky's *Theory of Poker*. Matt got more out of it than I did.

The Turn: Matt swapped strategy on Precambrian online forums like rec.gambling.poker and, later, Twoplustwo.com, where Sklansky held court. PartyPoker .com and PokerStars.com were the hunting grounds for rubes. Televised poker, such as *World Poker Tour*, captured the Real Deal for pause and rewind.

And, finally, the River: He finished writing *The Making of a Poker Player* just before he leveraged a satellite to the Final Table of the WPT 2004 Championship, and took home $700,000. All postscripts should come so easily.

The Making of appeared in 2005, squeezed into crowded Games & Amusements sections in bookstores. The gold rush was on, and proliferating how-tos were

◆

picks and shovels, crucial gear. Cardoza Publishing, the home of *Super System*, had enjoyed a 1,000 percent increase in sales the two years prior. Two Plus Two went from selling 45,000 books a year to half a million. (Dropping a lot of numbers these last few pages, but poker's a numbers game. How much, how many, baby.) Matt adjusted to the post-Moneymaker ecology of the game, and tech continued to provide an angle. He coached players over the phone, instant message, and e-mail, whatever your fancy. Narrated online training videos—wherein the Matt Himself mixed it up in computer tourneys while deconstructing his strategy in different hands. All downloadable to your handy mobile device, if you want.

Our digital existence, in fact, had made our meal possible. I'd sent up a flare to alert people on Twitter re: my Vegas plans. Matt responded: "If you want poker help . . . I can translate poker language into lit-speak." Social media wasn't usually my thing, as it had the word "social" in it, but I'd taken to the platform after a personal tragedy. I had a cat, the cat died, and now what I used to say to my cat all day, I tweeted. It helped that 140 characters was roughly my preferred limit when it came to human interaction.

There was rarely a misfit shortage at a poker table, given the more or less stable misfit percentages at any gathering of Americans, so I was not surprised that Twitter was big among their clan. I followed Coach's list of poker notables, poker scholars, and sundry jackanapes. A disturbing field excursion into player anthropology for someone of my delicate sensibilities. Apart from the standard "here's what I'm eating" updates, your poker feed kept your crew back home apprised of how you were faring, night and day, whether it's a strafing run at the casino just over the county line or the Aussie Millions in Melbourne. "You are there!" Stack size, notes on the talent in the room, table temperament. They dispatched little digital carrier pigeons at the table after a tournament, on breaks, and even hand by hand.

Here's a typical volley from Matros crony Robert Hwang, or Action Bob. It's Day 2 at the spring WSOP gathering in Atlantic City:

Caesar's main event. 120K playing 1200-2400.
135 players left. 174K for first.

After the first day, he's up to $120,000 in chips. The blinds at this level are $1,200 for Small, $2,400 for Big. The field has been culled to 135, and the winner will make $174,000. Time stamp: 4:38 p.m. He's been playing for a few hours. Then comes this at 6:10 p.m.:

Lost 110K pot QQ<<KK. 60K at 1500-3K.

Hey, now! The blinds are up. A pair of Kings has Paul Bunyoned his stack. At home, or on the bus home from work, Action Bob's fans, enemies, and spam followers wait to see how it turns out. Rubbing lips to a rosary, sacrificing goats to Beelzebub. The Poker Gods, wherever they may be. Eighteen minutes later:

Busto. AQ<<77 for my last 20 blinds.

Cue the music from *The Untouchables*, when Sean Connery is bleeding out and Robert De Niro as Capone chuckles as he gets word in his opera box. "Ri-i-i-di, Paglia-a-a-a-ccio!" Action Bob razed by a pair of 7s, losing twenty times the Big Blind of $3,000, or $60,000. Which he just mentioned was the size of his stack.

A nice three-act play. His followers look up at the sky and shake a smartphone at the indifferent heavens, or indifferent hell, if they are more Beelzebub-oriented.

All June, up at 3:00 a.m. and paddling the insomniac's dinghy, I scrolled through Coach's Twitter list of poker players. Three a.m. EST was prime-time Vegas action. An early encounter: a tweet with a picture of a registration card for a $25,000 Heads-Up Event, and the words: *All reg'd. Time to eat some souls.* So I had soul-eating to look forward to on top of everything else. The fact that my soul was very "eat it now and you'll be hungry again in a hour" was no comfort.

Combine poker lingo and textspeak and you're deep in linguistic badlands. Check out this string of integers from Jon Eaton, a habitué of Coach's list and of whom I knew little apart from his gnomic transmissions: *Sb limp i chk t8hh in bb flop 7h9hx he bets 1k i r to 3.2 w 9 back he calls turn 4h chk chk riv offsuit 4 he chks i jam he calls n mucks.* My first translation was pretty off: "All around is Sadness and Despair. Who will Save us, to Whom do we look for safety? There is No One." Eaton's tweet was actually the digest of a single hand playing out between the Small Blind and Big Blind. I think.

Daniel Negreanu was one of the few players with a Q rating, after all the poker shows, cameos in flicks like *X-Men Origins: Wolverine,* and charming-bachelor duty on *Millionaire Matchmaker.* He surveyed the ebb and flow of his stacks, but also invited his followers into the occasional post-epiphany glow: *Happiness on a scale of 1–10, I'm about a 312 right now! Can't get this silly grin off my face :-) Life is good . . .* Mike Sexton, avuncular commentator on *World Poker Tour,* dropped knowledge: *Stu Ungar once said to me, "Sexton, always remember this: All two aces are good for is to win a small pot or lose a big one."* Amen.

Others weighed in on lifestyle issues. Kevin Saul, one of Coach's buddies, was a war correspondent. *My dealer smells so bad now, I'm seriously tempted to pull my bottle of cologne out of my bag and spray it straight up n middle of tbl.* And: *Attn borgata poker, dood in red brooklyn spicers hoodie is too cool to wash his hands after pissing.* "The chips is filthy."

Before my arrival, I puzzled over his repeated references to the "hooker bar." Was *hooker* slang for a high roller? Some rootin'-tootin' tobacco-spittin' super ace? Then one evening I sat down at a Rio bar next to a hooker and knew: This must be the place.

As the WSOP death march progressed, event by event, week by week, for every *LOL I'm here 2 crush u* tweet, there was a *Busted out of the Main Event. Getting in my car and driving back to AZ.* Middle of the night, hitting the blacktop in sadness, that's messed up. I would've enjoyed a little more Vegas before splitting. Hot rock massage. A fucking mud treatment at least. Open the pores. But Matt keyed me into the pro mentality. "If you're trying to win it," he said, "it doesn't really matter how many days you're in it for. You're trying to get as many chips as you can, and if you get knocked out in the first couple of hours, it's really the same thing as getting knocked out on the third day, 'cause you didn't make any money either way."

Okay: Don't worry about the war chants on social media, and concentrate on rallying my meager skills for tomorrow. Leave the five-dimensional poker thinking for my betters.

At the time, I didn't know how my own Twitter feed would save me on Day 2.

HOW ARE YOU
GOING TO
BREAK IT TO CUJO?

In a corner of the Pavilion, the last-chance dance continued. The Noble Hustle, behind velvet ropes. Since September there had been Moneymaker-worthy satellites to transport you to the Main Event, underwritten by online sites and hosted by official WSOP circuit events in Biloxi, Council Bluffs, all over. Your local casino sponsors 'em, to lure you in for some ancillary losses. Even on Day 1C, there was still time for these hoboes to hop on the freight before it pulled away. Grind. Fail. Grind better. No way to know which one of these last-chancers I'd play with tomorrow. They were in the scrum, working.

Next year, June 2012, I came back to Vegas to see where it all began. You'll permit me a little time travel, buddy, this far into our journey. I'm not such a disagreeable companion, am I? Changing the cassettes, drawing my finger across the map to see we're headed in the right direction. By now I'm that old friend of yours, your fuckup friend, the one you love dearly and need desperately because he makes you feel better about your own disasters. Stick around for the usual denouement.

By the time the WSOP returned, I hadn't played a tournament in a year, for reasons that will become obvious. But I came back anyway, to watch Coach battle her way into the Big Game.

I bumped into her and her hubby, Lex, at check-in. Turned out we were on the same flight. They were giddy. According to real-time poker blogs and Twitter, twenty-seven-year-old Amanda Musumeci had smashed 'n' grabbed her way to the Final Table of Event 9, No-Limit Hold'em Re-Entry. Team Murder in effect. What's Team Murder? "Team Murder is this crew out of New Jersey," Coach explained. Okay. If Musumeci took it, she'd be the first woman to win a bracelet since Vanessa Selbst's 2008 win.

Musumeci eventually placed second, but it was a positive development. It had been seventeen years since a woman made it to the Final Table. The game was overdue.

In a few months, Selbst would become the top-earning female poker player of all time, with more than seven mil in earnings. "Tough as a Denny's porterhouse," as *World Poker Tour* host Mike Sexton put it. She first got her hands dirty online, where, according to James McManus's estimation, women make up 30 percent of the players. As opposed to the brick-and-mortar World Series, where that number was 5 percent.

Gender parity in poker is a joke. Walk into any card room, cue up any poker telecast, and the only place where you'll find a majority of women is on *World Poker Tour*, thanks to the show's Royal Flush Girls. Hey there, Brittany, Danielle, and Tugba! The girls are "event ambassadors" wafting past the camera between hands. In bikinis by the pool, and waving to the folk at home during a pleasant gondola ride down Venetian canals. Venice, Copenhagen, Prague—dude, that's why they call it the *World* Poker Tour. It's nice to have a job that lets you travel a lot and meet interesting people. With the addition of the Royal Flush Girls Social Media Bar, you can catch the girls in the background of the studio, perched on stools, small-talking with lucky members of the audience. "Bring your A game, fellas," Sexton advised.

Helen and Lex's excitement over Musumeci's run was in addition to the standard going-to-Vegas euphoria. They'd given themselves a week to come up with the Main Event money, whether it was from satellites, a couple of Deep Stacks, or robust cashes in $1,500-tier games. You need cash, and that ever-dwindling currency that always falls through a hole in your pocket: Time. Across the WSOP's six-week run, players cashed in their personal days and one-week's paid in search of the Big Score. "You'll have to go to trial without me—here's my

PowerPoint on 'Why the Death Penalty Is Bad.'" Missing Junior's Li'l Pelé Soccer Championship and Aunt May's fiftieth wedding anniversary.

If the cards behave? These plucky souls will have to come back in July, take an unpaid week, fake their kidnapping or the paperwork for glue-sniffing rehab. Shoot, they'll quit their jobs when they Final Table, anyway, all that money. This is not to minimize the tortured negotiations with significant others over another poker trip. With pets. How are you going to break it to Cujo? That Chihuahua has a lot of heart, but these absences take a toll.

None of that for Coach. Her partnership was poker-positive. They made a nice picture at the tables, Helen and Lex, rebuking the "I tuck my T-shirt into my jeans without a belt" crowd with her decorous ensembles and his fitted sports jackets and dress shirts. Table image: Nick and Nora, not Bud and Wheezie. Lex was taking a furlough from his day job as a writer and editor of business news. Said job which had added benefits: Lex served on his company's Diversity Committee and the annual Unity: Journalists for Diversity conference was in Vegas this August. They had a legit, societally acceptable excuse to come back, whether they cashed or not.

This trip they were beginning with a three-day event, Six Handed Hold'em. "The game that started it all," as

Helen put it, referring to her Phil Ivey–James Akenhead match two years prior. Maybe it's lucky.

At starting time, Coach was cozy at Bronze 61, Brasilia Room. It was the first time I'd seen her play. She wore a black dress with a white collar, pearl bracelet on her wrist. Legs crossed, vivid red nail polish glinting. Her fingers lightly brushed the table, as if she were in a canoe, her hand dipping lazily in the current. If this was her housewife costume, this day she was hosting a dinner party for some swell couples from the planned community, the roast cooling on the rack. If you check out the director's cut of *Rocky* this is exactly what Burgess Meredith wears when he gives his "A Bum's a Bum" speech in the deleted "Perfect Ham Sandwich" scene.

She patted the red purse in her lap: Let's go. When the cards flew, her table waited on one player, some hotshot who was tearing up shit in another event in the next ballroom. Or just some guy filling his Velcro pockets with protein bars and Pepto tablets at the sundries shop down the hall. At present, her adversaries were two young guys plugged into devices, one of the Ubiquitous Loquacious Middle-Aged White Guys, and a tattooed man with a sinister air. Yeah, I know your mom has a tattoo of Simon Le Bon on her back, but this was something else, a rather impressive wrist-to-shoulder ornamentation, "sleeves" they're called. Which seems a misnomer because generally one of the main things I look for in sleeves is remove-functionability.

Familiar types from my training missions at first glance. But no, their postures were more controlled, their expressions more rigid, their movements less slack. Versions of people I'd been playing against, impurities removed. The higher stakes, the cleansing fires of these hallowed WSOP halls, had burned away the weak stuff. What was still familiar: They could outplay me.

Let's patrol. Sixteen hundred runners entered Event 16, spread out among the convention hall. In other parts of the ballrooms, earlier matches wound down to the final, inevitable All Ins. Over in the Amazon, for example, it was Day 3, Level 70 of the $10K Heads-Up game, ESPN capturing one of the final tables for posterity. In the Pavilion, PokerNews.com streamed Day 2 of the $1,500 Limit Hold'em event, beguiling some thirteen-year-old in Punxsutawney with visions of future bracelet glory.

Early in the series, the population was sparse, the Main Event mob yet to curl into a fist. This locomotive was slow to accelerate. Fewer concessions hawking away in the corridors. The "misting station" on the terrace, which cooled the flesh from the desert's heat, was devoid of basking enthusiasts. The terrace: I loved it for its respite from the intense poker frequencies inside the convention hall. Even if the heat shriveled me like a piece of *charqui*, or jerky. (*Charqui*, "cut into strips and dried," from the Spanish, and the Incans, who dehydrated llama meat in the sun to preserve it.) A nice sprint through the misting-station jets sets you right.

The iPad population was up this year, however. In the Pavilion I caught one character squinting at an action scroller between hands, Beats by Dre headphones beeping in his ears. The Pavilion was where Lex was installed. Relaxed but alert in his dapper sports coat, some color in his angular face from his time at VooDoo Beach. Helen enjoyed a nice spa treatment before a big game; Lex didn't mind catching some rays at the Rio pool.

I tried to find Matt, but he was fathom deep at a table far from the velvet rope. I could just see him when his neighbor leaned back. Matt looked a bit flushed in his sweatshirt. Earbuds screwed in, concentrating on whatever holographic poker abstraction he projected into the air above the felt.

Then I was compelled to the satellite grottos, the Sit-n-Go's. Sit-n-Go's were not, as I had mistakenly thought, adult diapers for poker players, so they don't have to leave the table. Who wants to miss getting dealt aces? They're actually one-table, ten-player tournaments. Which explained a lot, like that time that floor manager kept shouting, "The Sit-n-Go is full! No more room in the Sit-n-Go!"

At our first meeting the year before, Coach had

◆

instructed me to hit some Sit-n-Go's during my AC training. But time was tight and I never did, concentrating on longer, protracted tournaments instead. When I told Matt at our lunch that I might warm up for Day 1D with a few, he shook his head. Why bother at that point? It was a different game than what I'd be playing in the Main Event. Different rhythms, different goals. It was too late.

Now I was fixated. See, something wonderful had happened the day before. In the cab to the Rio, Coach and Lex asked me if I was going to play. Naw, just take notes. Grateful to be a passenger again, after last year's ordeal. But an hour after I dropped off my bags, I was leching outside the Sit-n-Go's. Bunch of other pervs flitting around in anticipation, too. I wanted to play. Just one game.

The floor guy shuffled cards with different table stakes—125, 175, 200 smackers. Employing their idiosyncratic gambling spider-sense, the hopefuls registered for stakes that possessed the aura of good fortune. I recognized that feeling I first got in roller rinks and at high-school parties/shame cauldrons, where I'm going to dance but the song isn't right. I need the right one, some beat-box/synth concoction devised by weirdos. This one is too slow. This one is too corny—and then Prince comes on. I laced up and skated to a $125 table. After a few rotations, I saw it was the cheapest.

The order of business was simple: ten seats, ten players, winner takes all. I was rusty, but after an hour of "Do I cut the green wire or the red wire?" it was down to me and an older white guy. He was in a rush: Want to chop? Split the take? We shook hands.

I was up $490, and my old friend down in the utility room flipped the switch: *More.* The rest of the night I told myself I was done. The next morning, too. But how was I supposed to kill some time while Coach and Lex ran through their levels? I was almost done reading *I Wish I'd Never Had You: The Best of "The Family Circus."*

The word *More*, and also this bat-shit incantation over crazy-clown music: *Gonna do it, take 'em down, grab the pot, win it all.* Summon the waitress for a BAVERGE: self-delusion, neat. *Gonna do it.* I'm a fucking Sit-n-Go Master, I shoulda been playing these tables all along. My lucky number was $125. I played those stakes again. Lost. Back on the dance floor. Played $175—I won $490 at a $125 game, so if I win a $175 table, I'd pocket that much more. *Take 'em down.* It'll make up for that $125 I just lost. Plus, I'm still ahead from that one win, so the game I just lost doesn't really count. That's a natural dip. Up, down, that's how it goes, don't sweat it. *Grab the pot.* Those crazy clowns are really going nuts on that xylophone! Lost another $175. Cool. Still ahead. I'm not the only one doing this nutty tango, with this frenetic monologue running in my head. There's that scruffy Robotron with the backpack, and that woman in the baggy hoodie who nods at me when I play with her again, we're pals now. Oh—she's out again. She hit another Sit-n-Go the next table over. *Win it all.* I lose $175. Again $175. Again $175.

Stop.

This is insane. Feels great.

I should probably see how Coach is doing.

Whistling the Cold Deck Blues. Whittled down to $1,200 in chips, Perma-Sleeves on her left using simple gravity to suck chips to his person.

At break, Coach was vexed. Shaking her head. She told me about the pink note card she kept in her red purse for consultation in the bathroom: a list of dos and don'ts, her strategies and weaknesses set down by typewriter keys. Old-school. "And I just did that!" she said, referring to some unspecified prohibition. "It's a tough table. I can go All In, but it's going to be expensive."

Gosh. If I had Magic Negro hands, I could touch her chips, multiply them in a flurry of sparks. But I didn't have Magic Negro hands. Just hand hands.

"I've been in tougher spots," she said.

Across the afternoon and a succession of table breaks, Matt had drifted farther and farther from the rails. I got a glimpse of him grinding. We arranged dinner by text. Him and some Math Players, at Martorano's in the Rio.

Some of his pals were partaking of the Six Handed

downstairs, others taking a day off. Picking their shots, sticking to their lucky games. Appetizers before the main course. Today I fancied myself some sort of Sit-n-Go monster because of one chopped pot—well, imagine how you feel toward a game after taking home hundreds of thousands of dollars. Matt's posse returned to the WSOP salivating over this year's $10K H.O.R.S.E. or the $5K Limit outing, predisposed by previous outcomes. This shirt got me laid last time, it's sure to work again.

The Math Players had all cashed in the WSOP, in the Main Event or its preamble. Some, like Matt, had bracelets back home in the wall safe after winning events. Bill Chen, co-author with Jerrod Ankenman of the dense, next-level treatise *The Mathematics of Poker*, won the Six Handed in 2006, and bagged the $3K Limit Hold'em event the same year. He was sitting with Mike Fong in Martorano's when I introduced myself as Matt's friend.

Mike looked at Bill. "Isn't it pronounced, MAY-TROSE?"

Bill nodded. Yes, I'd been saying Matt's name wrong. Their game philosophy emphasized solid foundations: Why start dinner with a faulty premise?

Mike wasn't playing today. Chillaxing at Math House. Profiled in a 2010 ESPN article called "The Smartest House in Vegas," Math House was their HQ when they convened for the six weeks of the World Series. Swimming pool and a hot tub if the right rental popped up. Which made this the Smartest Table at an Overpriced Italian Restaurant in Vegas, but for my presence, which dragged the IQ level down to your average tailgate in the parking lot of an Albuquerque roller-derby match after an all-day whippit party. Which are fun, just not overflowing with the gifted.

"WSOP is summer camp for internet dorks," they told ESPN. Math House's first incarnation was a room at the Rio in 2005. Six weeks in a hotel gets pricey. That math I could get my head around, as I spend a lot of time figuring out what I'd do if I had to go on the lam after witnessing a mob hit, or to flee intimacy. Then the boys scoped out joints with enough bedrooms to hold their gang: Matt, Bill, Mike, and the others who joined us for dinner, Terrence Chan, Matt Hawrilenko, and Kenny Shei. They had encountered one another's screen names on theory-heavy boards like rec.gambling.poker, and got chummy in real-life casinos, drawn together by common card philosophy.

They lived all over the country, supporting themselves on poker or brain-busting jobs with titles like "strategic arbitrage." The annual hangout allowed them to catch up, trade strategy, escape the gastronomical perils of the Strip, and engage in that holy ritual of poker players: the Replay.

The Replay. Everyone did it. Home players shouting back to the table when they got up for another beer, know-it-alls haranguing strangers in a casino cash game, pros kicking back between wars. What would you have done? How would you have played it?

The Replay wants to know, What if I hadn't stepped on that butterfly? The one you crushed when you went back in time and then when you returned to the future everything had changed into something horrible. George Bush is in his fourth term, Diet New Coke the number-one pop in the land, and someone has invented "untethered telephones," entirely cordless, so people can just call you up whenever they want, to talk about whatever stupid shit pops into their heads. Some butterfly!

A million alternate realities branch off from that botched play, but with the Replay you can correct the mistake and set history straight. Find the world where you survive to the next level, pump up the old blood sugar at dinner break, and go on a tear to win the National Championship. What if you'd bet the pot in Barcelona, mucked in Tahoe, shoved in Choctaw, had never stepped on that bug? Un-step on that little bastard and you finally get what you deserve: ESPN zooms in on your harem as they cheerlead from the rails of the Final Table; Jack Link's retains you as a celeb spokesman in a series of post-ironic commercials; and a dozen bracelets spin on the special custom-made glass display in the master bedroom. Look:

You're putt-putting down the marble hallways of your McMansion on a limited-edition Ferrari-branded Segway, about to add another bracelet to the trove.

Lay your failures on the slab, let's gather around to check out the entrance wounds. The Replay cannot exist without an audience so you put it to the learned assembled: What do you do? Scientific, but sometimes this review resembled the probe of a tongue on a rotten tooth, or a neurotic's resurrection of primal hurts. I can remember a few botched hands—in between bites, Matt and his crew mulled over missteps from *years* back. That Deep Stack at the Bellagio in '09, Day 2 of the '06 WPT Championship. Supervillains they battle from time to time at this or that Million Dollar Game—how do you defeat his heat vision, her force field?

I tried to keep up.

"Do you call? I don't know."

"I lasted one level today."

"I lasted *one hand* yesterday."

"How'd you go out on Jacks?"

"He makes it a thousand—now what do you do?"

"What did he look like?"

"Fortyish white guy, nondescript."

Perfect disguise!

"From a value standpoint, you can fold to the—"

"Are you getting much of this?" Matt asked.

"Not at all."

I would never understand the game the way they did, no matter how much I studied and hit the tables. The part of the brain these guys used for cards, I used to keep meticulous account of my regrets. So many to sort and catalogue. Like when I meant to DVR the final episode of that reality show *The Last Time I Was Happy*, where contestants are interviewed on their deathbeds about the titular moment, the "winner" being the person with the longest dry spell. The hockey game ran late, and it only taped the first twenty minutes. I never found out who won. And that time upstate when I stumbled on an antique store where everything looked as if it had been left out in the rain. I like to buy furniture that reminds me of myself, I don't know. The store had a vintage nineteenth-century posture harness for sale, the kind with the mother-of-pearl adjustment knobs and leather braces, and I was sure it would straighten me out despite the condemnations of the so-called medical establishment. I went back the next day and it was gone. Never hesitate when it comes to nineteenth-century posture harnesses. And when I left for the World Series of Poker without hugging the kid one more time. That was a big one. These things add up.

That's why I had so much trouble storing all the new poker lore from books and conversations and time at the tables: no room. Given the choice between tracking real-life bad beats and poker-table bad beats, poker jockeys pick the more lucrative endeavor. They don't give gold bracelets for regrets.

In America.

There was one moment of intersection, when the topic of hate-watching came up. "Why do you watch TV shows—and keep watching them—if you don't like them?" Terrence asked.

Simple: Some days, all you have is gazing upon horror, and the small comfort of being surprised that it is not yours.

Middle of summer, but you could hear the leaves rustling. There was a hint of autumn as they reminisced. The specter of death, and not just from the cholesterol grenades coming out of the kitchen. The Math Players were cutting back on the poker, moving on. Mike was starting a new computer business in Cambridge. Matt Matros missed his wife, plus he had a novel to bake. He didn't stay the full six weeks anymore. Matt Hawrilenko would announce his retirement after this WSOP, sucked up by the Great Whale of grad school, before which so many were but drifting plankton.

Terrence, for his part, had been concentrating on his new mixed-martial-arts career. You know, Brazilian jujitsu, Muay Thai boxing, Western boxing and wrestling, things of that sort. The dude was cut. That mind-body problem I attempted to solve in my sessions with Kim Albano? Terrence had found the answer. As he explained in the PokerListings.com webvid about his course correction: "Even though it's maybe physically unhealthy to take a lot of blows to the face, it's in a way very spiritually healthy, and it really teaches you a lot about yourself."

Life! What Inscrutable Card Shall Ye Throw Next Upon the Soft Felt of Our Days? Six weeks plus six weeks plus six weeks: a section of your life lived in Vegas. Weeks that accumulated into a year under the accursed fried-chicken-joint heat lamp that is the desert sun. It aged you. The boys were getting on, some of them were even in their late thirties. "I'm routinely the oldest player at the tables," Matt said.

"We were the youngest, now we're the oldest," Kenny affirmed. Robotrons to the left of me, Robotrons to the right.

The check arrived and they made a deck for credit-card roulette. How it worked was you shuffled the cards, pulled one out, and its owner picked up the entire tab. "You don't have to if you don't want to," Matt said. I didn't. Lose this one, it's okay, we're all friends here, it evens out over time. Over these six weeks. Or the next time they play in AC or at Foxwoods. Next year's WSOP. If they came back. It's not like it used to be.

Then it was back to work. The next level of Event 16 awaited. I said goodbye to the Math Players on the floor of the Rio, at the head of the corridor that led to the convention hall. The other runners streaming past us back to

♦

the tables. One of my dinner companions invited me on a strip-club excursion. I demurred, spoiled by the erotic revues of Anhedonia, where the performers remain fully clothed but get emotionally naked, delivering monologues about their top-shelf disappointments, and times when they were almost happy. Hard to enjoy American-style strip clubs after that. Once you go bleak, you never go back.

The cards were in the air again. Thirty-seven minutes into Level 6, I checked on Coach.

There was an empty seat.

We all go out sooner or later.

I was back in NYC when Event 16 finally ended two days later. Hitting refresh-refresh on PokerNews.com, grabbing livestream bits on my phone while I walked down the street.

"Matt Matros is a Yale graduate. He's working on a novel," said Announcer #1.

"He's also a very sweet guy," said Announcer #2.

Matt was still in, ensconced at the Final Table when I got on the subway. When I emerged at street level, he'd won his third bracelet and half a million dollars. "It's beyond incredible, it's ridiculous," he told *PokerNews* correspondent Kristy Arnett, who interviewed him at his winning seat.

"You sound very humble, but come on," Kristy said. "Three years in a row. You're one of three people to ever do it in the last thirty years. Obviously, you're doing something right."

"I'm not saying I don't play well—I do. But I've been incredibly lucky these last three years at the Rio." He paused. "And my dad wants everyone to know my name is pronounced MAYTROSE."

Foundations. Master the foundations, and let us proceed from there.

....

Another jump: six months later. December 2012, Atlantic City. You with me? I drove down with Matt to sample circuit season. The six weeks of the World Series are one season, and the circuit tournaments, Poker Tour pit stops, and assorted megacasino events are another. Maybe you stick to the East Coast, or the Deep South, or never stray east of the Rockies, but you're on the hunt nine months of the year, whether you're a guru pocketing Player Points and big cashes, or a first-timer just learning the ways of the Noble Hustle.

It was raining on the trip down, the sky depleted of color. Matt was wrung out as well. After snagging that bracelet in last summer's WSOP, he was only hitting two or three fall events, a handful in the spring. Cutting back. He'd had a nice run, as usual. Since he started playing big tournaments, there'd only been two occasions when he was down for the year. Still tired, though. "I'm not tired about poker concepts and new ideas and discussing poker with other really good players," he said. "I still enjoy that aspect of it." But parking your butt in brick-and-mortar tournaments when you know what everyone's going to do before they do it? When there's only ten minutes every two hours when you're using your brain? It's dull, man. "I always wanted to try professional poker for a little while. I didn't think I was still going to be doing this when I was thirty-five. This is not supposed to have worked out as well as it has."

He'd rather be home with his wife, Ivy, instead of dragging his ass up and down the northeast corridor again. Rather write, work on his novel. He'd been knocking out his monthly column for *Card Player* magazine. Sample topics: "Think the Unthinkable, Do the Unthinkable: What Makes Great Players Great?" and "America's Love of Bluffing." Also on the agenda: agitating for the return of online poker in *Washington Post* op-eds. The only time I saw Matt get tilty was when he talked about the criminalization of his cherished cards.

Online poker excised the dull parts. Everyone had bad runs when they lost twenty tournaments in a row. "Tournament poker is high variance, as we say." You're up, down, and the number of bodies in a large tourney meant you weren't going to cash every time. No matter how good you were. But play thirty tournaments online a day, and those bad patches were truncated instead of stretching over a tortuous year.

The Illegal Gambling Business Act "was enacted in 1970 to crack down on organized crime," he wrote in the *Post*. "It was never intended to prevent ordinary people from playing poker." Unlike, say, craps, poker is a game of skill, he argued. A constant assessment of risk versus reward. Like Wall Street. If it were as random as roulette, good players wouldn't make more money than bad players over time. But they do.

Fighting the government was hard work—the Anhedonian Embassy had been disputing $60K in jaywalking tickets for years, cultural misunderstandings and whatnot.

"Our government disdains a risk-reward game that millions of Americans play," Matt wrote, "then bails out Wall Street sharks who bet unfathomable sums. I can only conclude that this contradictory stance has little to do with the skills required for each pursuit. No, for some reason, lawmakers just don't like poker."

Not that online lacked regrettable qualities. Collusion: How do you know that faceless users Bustanut69 and Lickylicky aren't scheming with each other on the phone, or sitting in each other's laps? That was an example of user misbehavior. On the other side of the screen, the moderators of Ultimate Bet abused their sys-op privileges to peek at players' hands and go pirating. "It was completely obvious they were a bunch of crooks," Matt said, "and anyone who played there was out of their minds."

Ultimate Bet faded, and Full Tilt Poker emerged with their own brand of mercurial ethics. They'd permit users to hit tourneys before their funds cleared and wager with cash they didn't have. With credit cards. Some of the money was vapor. Vapor or no, it circulated. Affiliate programs rewarded those who brought new fish to the site. More money spreading around. It didn't help matters that Full Tilt neglected to keep a firewall between the company's operating funds and players' money. The biggest rake in history. How did the owners spend this big pile of cash? The usual story: fancy cars, fancier women, beef jerky.

Then came Black Friday. The Feds put the kibosh on all online operations but saved their choice indictments for Full Tilt. According to the government, the company—fronted by some of the biggest names in poker, the dudes who had inspired most of these online players to take up the game in the first place—had defrauded its users out of $300 million. "Sorry, your account has been frozen." Matt knew people who'd had 70 or 80 percent of their bankroll tied up in the electronic ether—gone. Hundreds of thousands of dollars. Paper millionaires, teenagers who'd never had a bank account in their life, reset to zero. Middle-aged guys grinding sixty hours a week, supporting their families on the fifty grand they eked out each year, were suddenly without jobs. That's how they paid their mortgages, with a full house here and river bluff there.

The national recession had caught up to organized poker. There was dark talk about suicides. Rumors. No one really wanted to talk about it. Eighteen months after Black Friday, a lot of that money was still in the hands of the government, who wanted to get paid first before they tackled the matter of reimbursements.

Adapt or die. Just as the cowboys had to readjust to the young gunslingers and their new loose-aggressive poker or hang up their holsters, the Robos needed to learn to handle brick-and-mortar casinos. As we drove to AC, Matt's disquisition on the State of Poker Today darkened the already overcast sky.

This Harrah's circuit event was eleven days long, with twelve big-ticket games and assorted remora Mega Satellites and Turbo Mega Satellites. The biggie this weekend was the $1,600 buy-in Main Event. Some six hundred regional players hopping on buses, driving down, getting a ride with Mom. The prize pool just shy of a million dollars.

Helen and Lex were there, too. Friday night they were playing a $200 Mega Satellite to chute into Saturday's biggie. As usual, the top 10 percent of the satelliters got a ticket to next day's event. Months earlier, Coach and her hubby had failed to make it into the WSOP Main Event. Now, in winter, the carousel had started up again. Like the thousands of poker legions across the world, they hoped to be in Vegas when the music stopped.

Okay—I'd been spoiled by the show-biz accoutrements of the Main Event. The TV cameras, the B-list celebs, the Poker Kitchen. Harrah's Atlantic City WSOP stage was your typical meeting space in a mid-price hotel, windowless and dingy. Today it's poker. Next week it'll be a Chia Pet regional sales conference, a franchise meeting for Bespoke Snuggies, or an all-day Just Be Yourself self-actualization seminar, for which the doors will probably be chained shut until you sign up for the pricey Steps 1–12 workbooks. Bonus if you bring a friend, like Full Tilt.

The Final Table of Event 7, No Limit Hold'em, unfolded on a tiny area cordoned by scuffed brass rails. For Just Be Yourself, that's where participants will beat each other with foam bats while screaming "Can you hear me now, Mommy!," but the action now was droopy-lidded. The long slog. I plopped down in the modest audience seats while the satty players queued up to register. They were young and scruffy, day bags slung over their shoulders. They might be crashing overnight and playing tomorrow—or heading home in an hour. It had been a long time since I'd been in the presence of non-Vegas players. These guys, I recognized them by their groans.

After a crappy meal downstairs, Helen and Lex grabbed their table draws. Slim food picking on this side of Harrah's, but they had enough fuel to get them to midnight. If they didn't bust.

As usual, they classed up the joint. Lex joined his table in a smart charcoal jacket and blue oxford. Coach opted for posh-ninja mode, black sweater and black pants. Only the moonlight glinting off her red fingernails would give her away, as she garroted mofos amid the mounting levels. Like the fanny-packed, beer-gutted others filling the tables, Coach and her husband wanted to place at the top of the satellite and keep the 1,600 bucks for Event 10 in their pockets. Would they fork it over if they didn't make it tonight? The eternal calculus of the Noble Hustle, where bankroll meets the reality of how the cards are running. I watched one hopeful pad around in a daze after being flushed out of the 5:00 p.m. Mega. He walked to the doors, walked back. Still time to enter the 7:00 p.m. satellite. "Do I want to do this again?" he said aloud.

He hiked his bag on his shoulder and reenlisted.

I caught up with Matt in a Bobby Flay joint over in the Borgata, where we dined with Action Bob and Lana O'Brien. Bob was the star of the three-act tweet-play I related earlier. He lived in nearby Barnegat, New Jersey, with his wife and kids. Typical modern dad. When his family sleeps, he'll come to the plush Borgata Poker Room and play $40/$80 Limit, rising early every weekend to fleece the "tired, drunk, angry" who have been playing all night and are trying to get even. "It's worth getting up at five," he said with a grin. Play in the morning, he can hang out with the fam in the afternoon.

Lana was a young colleague of Matt's from Card Runners.com, the poker academy. Currently Matt's apprentice and trying to step up her game, although time was running out. She was pregnant with her second kid and starting to show. Maternity leave from Hold'em loomed. If the online sites were up, she could telecommute, but . . .

Lobster and Crispy Squid Salad. Amid the Flaying, Matt, Lana, and Action Bob partook of the Replay. Dug into the archives, recalling a multitude of crime-scene variables—position, stack size, the opponent's preferred range of hands. Crucial points of personal history—was that before said supervillain stopped drinking, or where they were still an ogre at the table? The action sequences of their poker movie, on slow-mo to admire the F/X work. The supporting cast had taken their marks last month at the Fall Open, and would return to deliver their lines next month at the Winter Open. Character actors too colorful to be out of work long.

How did they keep track of it all? Those old battles.

Action Bob shrugged. "You get used to it." He checked his watch. He had to leave the table for a few minutes, to call home but also for face time at his $40/$80. Dinner break, yeah, but he had to pop in for two hands so he didn't lose his seat. His kids gotta eat, too.

Wild Mushroom Mashed Potatoes with Truffle Oil, Spice-Rubbed Rib Eye. A nice steak before they played tomorrow at Harrah's. No satellites for them. The numbers didn't work out. Why spend ten hours grinding when the 1,600-buck entry fee is just the price of doing business? A satellite for a $10K tourney was doable, in a time-money calculation. Not that they'd do it, but at $10K the numbers started to make sense. Sometimes you force down a Southwestern Chicken Wrap, next time it's steak. Bankroll is all.

Plus, satties are boring, they all agreed. You're angling to get into the top ten, not money. You play differently, the way you adjust for Six Handed versus a ten-seat game. "Fold, fold, fold, fold," Lana said, and wait for a good shot.

Better to eat a nice meal, rest up, and hope for a good table. "Last year, my opening table was the best I ever had," Action Bob said. Wistful.

"They were good players?" Must be exciting, entering into combat with your peers. A worthy challenge.

"He means, *great* meaning *bad*," Matt said. Like when Run-D.M.C. says, "Not bad meaning bad, but bad meaning good." May the Poker Gods gift us some terrible players, some real bozos, so we can make some money.

Lana wasn't entering Event 10 on Saturday, but the

Ladies Event that ran at the same time. She was down to play some cards. Eager and full of cheer. Since training with Matt, she'd achieved a new level in her play. "Whenever you can get up and play poker, it's a great day."

"I used to be like her," Matt said.

Back at Harrah's, 10:30 p.m. The satellite had dwindled to two tables, eighty-five gladiators culled to eighteen. And there were Helen and Lex, still in it. Sitting next to each other. Married couples were rare in poker. But here they were, might as well have been sitting on the couch back home, thanks to the accident of table breakage. It was adorable, but I didn't tell them that until the break. I didn't want to mess up their camouflage.

Coach was up to $38K, and Lex hanging on at $15K. Shove time for the man, once he picked his opening.

"Will you take Lex out if you have to?" I asked.

"Definitely," Coach said.

Lex smiled. "Ask us later about the Kings versus Aces story."

The game had decelerated, this close to the bubble. Bubble Boy, where art thou? Fold, fold, fold, fold. If Coach and Lex outlasted the next clutch of players, they were in tomorrow's $1,600 game. They ran alternative scenarios, like everyone else in the third-floor ballroom. If Lex busted, there was an 11:00 a.m. Turbo game, and if he cashed there, he could make the second, 7:00 p.m. start of Event 10. If that didn't work out . . .

Coach, for her part, might fork over for the Main if she crapped out tonight. The Ladies Event was cheaper, but the idea incensed her. "That's sexist!" she said. "I'm upset. They assume or whatever that women will not be in the Main Event—why else would they schedule it at the same time?" Yep, if the Mega didn't pan out, she'd pay her way in. She was still up for the year, cashes-wise. The price of doing business.

Lex busted out a few seats from the bubble, at fourteen.

He hit Replay and nodded to himself. "I think that was the right move." He joined me on the rails. To Turbo or not to Turbo?

Eighteen to fourteen to twelve seats. Almost there. At midnight Coach was up to $70K, battling.

I was tired. And I didn't belong. These people were scientists. I departed to play $2/$4 No Fold'em Hold'em downstairs with my people: the Methy Mikes, the shivering elderly, and the drunken fifty-somethings in town for AC shenanigans. Back with poker's hoi polloi, with our tepid raises and sloppy calls. Adele sang "Rolling in the Deep" and CeeLo crooned "Fuck You," just as they had during my Vegas WSOP jaunt a year and a half ago. The same pop songs still circulating, the communal soundtrack of a life half lived. It was safe down there with the dopes.

Outside Harrah's the next morning, a brief scene:

♦

Sedans and town cars double-parked, the valet is scurrying around trying to sort it out. A quartet of week-ending sixty-somethings, three men and one woman, mill around a white Honda. It's unclear if they are arriving or departing. We know why everyone comes here, but we all leave under different circumstances.

"C'mon, I want to gamble," says the man at the center of the tussle. Unsteady on his feet but full of energy. Bristling.

"You can't stand up," says one of his companions.

"C'mon," the belligerent old dude says. He gets one foot in the backseat of the Honda and then reconsiders. His companions have their hands on him.

"You'll fall again."

"C'MON. I WANT TO GAMBLE. GET A WHEELCHAIR!"

They continue to try and pack him in the car. The woman paces back and forth, a spouse unsure what her role is in this fight. Intervene or no, what are the repercussions? After all these years the same dilemma.

"C'MON! GET A WHEELCHAIR!"

I'd seen a lot of gambling in the last year and a half. Exciting gambling. Foolhardy gambling. Gambling as an art form. What this old dude enacted was fodder for the pamphlets and PSAs the casinos give you as they happily hand over chips. Another great gambling truth. But I'll leave that for other correspondents.

Later. Saturday afternoon, the kickoff of Harrah's Main Event. Lex was playing his Turbo. I found Matt, cheerful in his crimson zippy, and wished him luck. He was more upbeat than he'd been on the ride down, perhaps revitalized by his night playing Open Face Chinese Poker in an amigo's comped hotel room. It was a new game, the new cool hot rod among the gambling set, and it was his first time kicking the tires. Matt may have been burned out and preoccupied, but he perked up when he explained the rules. "You get dealt thirteen cards and you have to set your hand in such a way that your worst hand is a three-card hand in the front, then your second-best hand is a five-card hand in the middle, and then your best hand is a five-card hand in the back . . ." I had no idea what the hell he was talking about. But I was glad to see he still loved cards, despite his late uneasiness with success.

I cruised between the tables and discovered Action Bob ready for battle, with his Gigantor cup of Dunkin' Donuts coffee, sunglasses, and earbuds. He waved, grinning. Across from him sat Coach in a turquoise blouse with gold flower petals. Just another Saturday afternoon of cards with some of the neighbors on Oak Street.

I don't know if their table was bad meaning bad or bad meaning good, but the cards snapped and the gamblers hunkered, the million-dollar winners and the diligent grinders, the jowly veterans and the pimply first-timers.

Any one of them could win it all, and no one deserved it more than anyone else.

Let's leave them there, as they wait for the next hand, the one that will change it all. I have a game to return to myself.

What do you say we see what happened that one time I went to Vegas?

EVERY ANTE
IS A SOUL

Like my first sexual experience, my time at the World Series of Poker didn't last long . . . is how I would've started this section if I'd been eliminated the first day. But I wasn't. Suck it, Entropy. We have an appointment, my old friend, but not today.

I was up at 5:00 a.m. We have a saying back home: "Wake up in the grip of terror, things will get worse before they get better." (It is also the title of one of our most beloved children's books.) Scratch the wake-up call, which is no way to start the day, wherever you come from. Why so cold and distant, hotel robot voice? "This is your 6:00 a.m. wake-up call." What's wrong with "Go get 'em, Tiger!" or "You look sexy when you sleep"?

Dig if you will a picture: Sunday at noon. I was finally able to register after the accountants found my check. My table draw was Yellow 163, Seat 9. Pavilion. When I returned half an hour before start time, the room was mostly full, the players warily clocking their tables, approaching, backing off, like guests at a reception waiting for the signal to dig into the canapés. No one wanted to be the first to go out, and no one even wanted to be the first to sit down.

The announcer bid us to join the dealers, who had been at their stations, bow-tied and patient. Terse greetings all around. "Hey." "How's it going?" Mostly fifty-something white guys, with two youngsters in Seats 5 and 6. Yes, the young guys owned the game now—the past couple of winners have been under thirty. Some of them probably even did yoga.

They played "The Star-Spangled Banner." I stood out of politeness. One does not often hear the national anthem of the Republic of Anhedonia at a sporting event. The so-called "lyrics" consist mostly of grunts, half-muttered curses, and long, drawn-out sighs, depending on the particular sufferings you're cultivating that day. Still, it never fails to lift the spirit, however faintly, we agree on this if nothing else.

You don't want to see our flag, trust me.

Phil Hellmuth, superplayer from the Silver Age, and "Playmate Holly Madison" started the tourney with, "Shuffle up and deal!" The cricket orchestra started up. I wouldn't have minded "Shuffle through your mistakes and tremble!" but tradition is tradition.

The blinds were $50 and $100. One of the young

players at my table, the Guy in the Teal Hoodie, started off energetically. He had the demeanor of a college alt-rock DJ or someone building cybernetic organisms in the garage, and took down pots with quiet efficiency. Was he one of the *young players* Matt had warned me about the day before?

I'd asked Matt if he'd seen any "new moves" this year, the latest gizmos, which was very silly because I barely knew the old moves, whether we were talking Hold'em or the Cabbage Patch.

"These *young players*," he said, "they're four-betting with nothing. Five-betting." He said *young players* the way World War II grunts used to say *Hun bastards*. The Big Blind is considered the first bet, a raise on that is the second bet, and a re-raise on top of *that* is a three-bet. Pretty normal stuff before the flop, the first three communal cards. In his *Little Books of Poker*, Phil Gordon repeatedly warned, "Beware the Fourth Bet—it means Aces." Lemme tell you, son, in my day, four-betting used to mean something. Nowadays, these *young players* were four-betting, five-betting helter-skelter, who knew what these crazy kids had in their hands, they could be raising with shit, rags, 7-2. The preflop four-bet was a relatively new weapon in the arsenal, but that didn't mean I had to back down when I had decent cards. Matt told me to trust my instincts. "If you have a good read on someone, five-bet them. If they're bluffing, they'll fold." Okay! I told him I was going to play tight, try to make it to Day 3, not misplay my premium hands . . .

"Do you want to do that," Matt asked, "play it safe?" I was here to write an article, but was that all there was to it? "I think you'll be most satisfied," he said, "if at some point, you suddenly have a read on someone: 'This guy doesn't have anything' or 'This guy has something.' One way or another, you're going to have a read, and you're going to do something that you didn't expect you were going to do before, right or wrong." Something new in your game expressing itself. "Obviously it's better if you're right, but even if you're wrong, it can be really satisfying to just have a read, a feeling, and go with it. Your gut."

I could play it safe, or I could really *play*. Matt was asking me, Why are you here? It was the Vegas question, namely: What the fuck are you doing in Vegas? As usual in this town, whether you gambled away the mortgage money, fucked a stranger, or went to see Carrot Top, you answered in your actions.

There were three empty seats. Brighton Beach eventually sat on my left. He was an intense, twenty-something dude with a strong cut-off-your-feet-and-mail-them-to-your-fiancée vibe. Eventually Seat 8 showed up. The dealer looked at his ID and said, "Oh, shit!"

One thing you do not want to hear is a dealer say "Oh, shit!" when a player joins your table. He was wearing a red World Poker Tour jacket with . . . was that his name embroidered on the left breast? This motherfucker was so bad, he had a goddamned monogrammed World Poker Tour jacket! Floor managers and players from other tables moseyed over to say hello. He was on my right, and if he went crazy with six-betting or nine-betting or who knew what, I could make a quick muck. Horrified, nonetheless.

I had enough chips to withstand some hits, power in the forward deflectors. We started with $30K, 300 Big Blinds. Plenty of M. "It's all about M," Coach had told me during our initial training session, and it was one of the first things I came to understand, slowly, the hard way, during my AC runs, the secret narrative as I passed through levels. M is how much life you have in you, how much you can take. To calculate M, you add the Big Blind, the Small Blind, and all the antes you have to pay into the pot each round, and the sum is how much it costs to play one orbit 'round the table. M, for Paul Magriel, who first articulated it, but also M for the Wave of Mutilation.

Above 20M, twenty rounds, you can play your fancy-move poker. But once you dip below that, your spirit is draining away each round, and you have to start playing more aggressively, play a wider range of cards, swipe some blinds, so that you are not erased from existence. Existence, because this is life we're talking about here, how much can you take before you break. Dear reader, I hope you're operating at a big M most of the time, I really do.

Things are easier that way. But then sometimes things go wrong—you lose your job, get some sort of health issue named after a foreigner, the kid won't say why he doesn't want you at the wedding, and the angry voices in your head are now using Auto-Tune. You take a tumble in a thousand ways, big and small: This the Wave of Mutilation, gobbling up your reality. Replay the hand—is there something you could have done differently to keep things the way they were, something you should have said to keep them from walking away? It doesn't matter, the dealer's shuffling again. You dwindle to 6M and 3M and 2M and you can't pay the rent next month, nobody's returning your e-mails. Things are desperate. This is death. You don't know how you're going to survive. And the truth is, you're not going to. Next level, the blinds will go up, and up, and up.

That's M.

Seat 7 never showed and was blinded away until a floor manager removed the remnants of the stack. What came up for him or her to blow the $10K entrance fee? I hoped they were tied up in a dungeon somewhere. Not a serial-killer dungeon but one of the tony thousand-bucks-an-hour variety you can find only in Vegas, and they were having a pleasant time at the lashes.

Coach gave me a simple order for the first three levels: "Make it to dinner." You can sort players into dependable categories. *Tight* is conservative. *Loose* plays a lot of hands.

Loose-Aggressive plays a lot of hands, plays a lot of shit, but will bully you with betting. At the first table, I played something that might be called Tight-Incompetent. I folded out of turn, tried to bet 2.5x the BB, per the table custom, but misidentified the chips and put in less than 2x, which was a no-no. I made each mistake only once (for a change; see Dating Failures of, in my index for contrary indicators) but I'd marked myself as the weak player. At Yellow 163, I got my nicest run of cards, QQ, JJ, flopped an Ace-high flush, but there wasn't a lot of action. I wasn't down, but I wasn't fattening my stack.

I heard the cries from the other tables as All Ins began and people busted out. I saw my first right before the end of Level 1, when Brighton Beach, who was down to $10K, shoved. He was getting a massage. I'd seen someone on Coach's poker feed say that hubris is the short stack ordering a massage. Did I mention the masseuses? There were teams of them, ladies in white polos hoisting their cushions, rubbing lotion into hairy necks. Brighton Beach shoved his stack into the pot, and a minute later he was out. I wondered if his rubdown would be prorated. Everybody shook their heads and checked out their own stack. Chill wind as the Grim Reaper strolled past. Anyone could be next.

Level 1 ended. The line for the men's was a bit long, as Coach had warned. The smokers beat it out to the patio. I hadn't seen that many smokers in years. As I hustled back to my room, I googled the dude in the World Poker Tour jacket. He was Matt Savage, proselytizer for the New Poker. I'd been following his Twitter feed for weeks—as a director of pro tournaments and commentator on the TV show, he answered questions about rules and regulations. He wasn't Godzilla, but I was still glad to be downwind from his betting. In my room, I wrote some notes, reviewed my tip sheets, and made it back in time for Level 2. Breathe in, breathe out.

Enough people had busted that the floor managers started breaking up tables, rerouting players on the outskirts of the room to the empty seats at the center. Day 1D was a contracting, dying star. We gathered our chips and dispersed into the void. I saw Savage every once in a while during the following levels. We waved. The next time I spoke to the Guy in the Teal Hoodie, it was at the end of Day 6. I said hi, weirdly eager and proud that one of the fellows from the first table was still around.

"I remember you," he said, with a mellow drawl. "You were in Seat 9. You were a good player."

Too kind. "How are you doing? Still in?"

"I'm chip leader," he said. "I have 12.8 million." His name was Ryan Lenaghan, an online player who had discovered he liked casino play. He finished in eighteenth place.

....

My second table was Black 63, Seat 10. I have been invited to someone's house for Thanksgiving and arrived with my sweet potato pie in the aftermath of a big argument. What happened here? There's carnage everywhere. Two young guys would nurse $12K for the rest of the night, sober play that was a reversal of whatever had decimated them. Yeah, something big went down before I got there. Daddy's drinking again, Gabby got her nethers pierced.

No one seemed to like the loud Aussie in Seat 4. He'd raked some pots and when he left for cigarette breaks, everybody made fun of him. He looked like the cow-faced droog from *A Clockwork Orange*, completing the effect with a weird hat his shag peeked out of. The table captain was named Marc Podell. He was a fellow New Yorker in his early forties, and he made a steady accumulation for the rest of the day. He was getting cards—he had no problem showing us why the other guy should have folded—but he was also outplaying us. Half the time he was getting a rubdown (he knew the masseuse from Main Events past, they set up appointments by text), and the other half he was calling the raiser and showing the better hand. The Aussie was the other big stack at the table, and Marc tried to goad him into going on tilt. It worked.

"How many chips do you have?" I started hearing that a lot more, this locker-room check: Who has the bigger dick? It was posturing, but also a serious consideration of how many chips this would cost you if it went south. I got more JJs and played them, a pair here and there. It was a tight table. No one wanted to go home on the first day.

Some players sell "pieces" of themselves, where if you pay a percentage of their entrance fee, you get a cut of the winnings. If any. Whole online trading exchanges were devoted to this human capital. I wasn't too keen on buying and selling people—legacy of slavery and whatnot—and this lot struck me as guys who were gambling with their own money. I never saw a four-bet or five-bet. I was playing tight, too, and should have started running a bluff here and there now that I'd "established a solid image at the table," as they say in the books. But I held back. Establishing table image is like when you stab the leader of the Aryan Assholes in the neck with a fork your first day in prison: telling 'em how you do it back home.

I was still stuck in playing good cards well, don't get all crazy mode. I began running with my interpretation of Matt's reads, mixed in with some tidbits from *The Gift of Fear* by Gavin de Becker. Coach had told me to read it, after she'd heard about it on *Oprah*.

The Gift of Fear wasn't a poker book but a self-helper about identifying encounters that might escalate into violence. How do you know when someone is out to harm you? Use your animal intuition, developed by millions of years of evolution. Confronting a possible full house wasn't the same thing as being followed down a deserted street at night, but Coach had discovered poker applications: "When it comes to the game, your first instinct is usually right." Danger! Danger! Was it counterintuitive to apply lessons from a women's self-defense book to the World Series of Poker? Yes. But if modernity has taught us anything, it's that you don't fuck with Oprah.

Breathe in, hold it, breathe out. I made it to dinner, per Coach's order. Three levels. Her other order? "Go to the seafood place. Get the swordfish."

The line was too big, so I got some cruddy sandwich and ate at the Sports Book. I called Coach to debrief, told her about Matt Savage and the sleepy play at my first table.

"They're calling that section 'Mellow Yellow,'" Helen said, chuckling. She'd sworn off tournament news after her less-than-satisfying WSOP visit weeks ago. But now she was hunkered over her poker feed, reading players' tweets from the tables, checking out the competition: She had a player in the game.

Her order for Levels 4 and 5 was simple. Get Bagged and Tagged—crawl to the end of the day, write my name on a plastic bag, and drop my chips inside for safekeeping until Day 2B. It almost seemed possible. This horror show ran seven days. Early on, you wanted to stay cool and keep out of expensive confrontations, but you also needed to feed the stack. The stack is *hungry.*

◆

One of the players in my cheapo home game was Nathan, whose friend Steven Garfinkle was in town for the WSOP. A professor of ancient history at Western Washington University, Steven called himself a "committed amateur," as opposed to a pro, although plenty of pros wouldn't mind a tenth-place finish in the World Series, which is how far he made it in 2007. Yes, he'd fed his stack that year. "You can't win it the first day," Steven told me. But, he added, "You can't fold your way into money." You gotta play.

His stay was being comped by the Aria, one of the new Cosmo-style dreadnoughts moored in the City-Center complex. The Aria was more than twenty stories tall, a fortification dwarfing the old standbys of the Strip in the manner of the other upstarts. ("These *young players*," says Circus Circus, "they do it differently.") On the casino floor, tiny lights blinked in the walls, I walked on silvered floors, and techno music summoned me to this or that pleasure zone around the next bend. A real *Logan's Run* building—outside the walls, my world was ruined, the Library of Congress half buried in sand.

Inside Aria, however, everything was swell, except for the recent outbreak of Legionnaires' disease, which lent a "Masque of the Red Death" air to the proceedings. On the night of 1C, I tagged along for dinner at Jean Georges. Comped! I asked Steven what a good goal for the first day was.

A good day is tripling, he told me, but hitting the room's average is okay, too. There comes a point in the event, Steven said, when "The Big Blind is someone who was here." Day 6 started with a $30K Big Blind, which was how many chips you got for your buy-in. Thirty thousand to start off the hand, it represented a human soul who had looked at their table draw the first day and said, I feel lucky. Just like you had. And then there is a point, he continued, "when the *ante* is someone who was here." This was all that remained of a person, their buy-in, and the Final Table rolled them in their hands and tossed them to the felt. Like gods. Coach had said that her World Series time was "heaven," and here it was: the big pot as afterlife, containing the spirits of the eliminated players.

Take, for example, the tall, thin man in Seat 2, who arrived at Black 63 from a broken table. He had long dark hair and wire frames with light blue lenses. Throw in the black clothes, and if he declared that his job title was "Master of Illusions," taught Criss Angel all he knew, I'd have believed him.

He and Marc Podell, the guy who continued to command our table into the late hours, recognized each other from "around"—life in the circuit badlands. He was supertight, a clam's clam, this older gentleman. I couldn't really see him around the curve of the table, and he rarely played a hand, so I only paid attention to him when he mixed it up. Which he finally did a couple of hours after dinner break. He went for it—shoved All In before the flop. Marc called him. AA versus KK. Marc had the two Aces. The man went poof, rabbit in a hat.

"That was sad," I said. I don't think "sad" is a poker term, but there it was. I'd barely spoken all day except to say, "Raise." The Master of Illusion had been sitting so quietly for so long, mum, watching, waiting for precisely a hand like KK. KK—of course you're going to go for it. And just like that, he was atomized, called up to the Big Stack in the Sky.

"I've seen him play before," Marc said, grabbing the chips. "I knew he had something good." But not good enough for Marc's Aces. He casually mentioned that this day's haul might be larger than his starting day in 2008, when he cashed in hundredth place. He ran over the rest of the table, it was our fault. Spend that money, work at your craft for years and years and finally make it to the Main Event: People were scared. What are you going to tell them at the water cooler if you go out the first day? Poker studs loathe "nits"—tight-playing schlubs who never mix it up, only betting monster hands. A nit is a lowly person, and here we were, a nit infestation. But I knew this, too: We were nits who wanted to be men.

I was definitely taking a grifter's approach to my table image. This wasn't the long con, though—I should have loosened up my betting once I saw I was playing with a bunch of Tentative Johnnys.

But I didn't.

LEVEL 4: $27K

LEVEL 5: $23K

One improvement: mother hen-ing my blinds. I'd considered blinds and antes like income tax, what you have to pay to be a member of society. To fund pothole repair and corrupt, no-bid government contractors. But blinds are money. They are meaningful. They add up. Matt told me a lot of players nowadays preferred to use your number of Big Blinds in their actuarial tables of life expectancy, instead of M. After these crippling levels, I got it. There were two guys at Black 63 who were statues, except when targeting undefended Big Blinds. Swipers, after Dora the Explorer's klepto nemesis. They preyed on blinds, scavenging to survive. When the latest swiper joined our table, he had a big stack of green chips, the ante chips. "That's how you know," Coach had told me.

I noticed the pattern. I was folding too easily when I was Big Blind and held shit cards in my hand. The swipers had pegged me as an easy mark. The swiper on Marc's left—he kept farting or burping, from Marc's wrinkled-nose rebukes—perked up when he was on the button. My BBs were easy pickings.

I finally started playing back at him, shooing flies away from my hamburger in a crappy diner. He stopped.

Lesson: If you're going to view blinds as taxes, be a Republican about them.

Level 5 was over. We bagged our chips in ziplocks, wrote our names on the plastic. It was 12:45 a.m. I was a lump of quivering human meat, but somehow I'd made it through Day 1 with $23K. Half the average stack. The next day, the blinds would escalate to $250 and $500, with $50 antes. I whipped out the abacus: I was at 19M. On my way upstairs, I bought a pouch of Jack Link's Beef Jerky. No mere marketing ploy, the easy-seal bag really did lock in freshness.

I'd be back for Day 2B, if my own, personal daily Wave of Mutilation didn't wash me away first.

M

I keep mentioning jerky. On that first Vegas trip in '91, we stumbled on a wonderland.

It was a grubby spot on Fremont Street, just past the Four Queens and Binion's, embedded in an outcropping of souvenir shops. The House of Jerky. I knew Slim Jims, those spicy straws of processed ears and snouts. This was something else entirely. We squinted in joyful bafflement before the rows of clear plastic pouches filled with knobs of dark, lean meat, seasoned and cured. Li'l baggie of desiccant at the bottom for freshness. The jerkys reminded me of Anhedonia's ancient groves, specifically their tree bark, which we peel 'n' eat in times of drought and on major holidays. We walked the aisles. The flavors were ordinary, yes. Pepper, teriyaki, barbecue. But the ark-ful of proteins was miraculous: beef, Alaskan salmon, buffalo, turkey, alligator, venison, ostrich.

The proprietor was a middle-aged Asian man named

Dexter Choi. That one man's singular vision could beget such bounty! It was America laid out before us, dangling on metal rods set into scuffed particle board. Complete with wide open spaces, for the store had a modest inventory. Dried fruit. Nuts. But mostly jerky.

Mr. Choi remained unmoved by our oh-snaps and holy-cows. The House of Jerky was kitsch to us, but we stood inside the man's desert dream that day. You know there was a hater chorus when he shared his plans. "Forget about jerky, Dexter, study for the electrician's licensing exam." "Sure jerky is a low-calorie, high-sodium snack, Dexter, but when are you going to get your head out of the clouds?" "Look at these lips, Dexter—will your dried muscle-meat ever kiss you like I do?"

He endured. To build a House of Jerky is to triumph against the odds, to construct a nitrate-filled monument to possibility and individual perseverance. Dexter Choi was an outlaw. He faced down fate and flopped a full house.

Maybe things could have improved re: foot traffic, but I couldn't help but be moved. From that day on, beef jerky was synonymous with freedom and savory pick-me-ups between meals. We bought a few bags of that sweet bark for our drive into Death Valley and continued on our journey.

How could I foresee that this cowboy snack would become a symbol of corporate poker, indeed the commercialization of all Las Vegas? Beef jerky was now the leathery, mass-produced face of modern poker. Meat snacks generated $1.4 billion a year in business, Jack Link's a major player. Started in the 1880s by an immigrant named Chris Link, who served up smoked meats and sausages to Wisconsin pioneer folk, Jack Link's was now the fastest-growing meat snack firm in the world, with a hundred different products sold in forty countries. "More than a century has passed," the Our History page of their site announced, "but the Link family principles and traditions remain the same: hard work, integrity, and a commitment to earn consumer respect by delivering the best-tasting meat snacks in the world."

Respect them I did. Since 2008, the company had been an official sponsor of the Main Event—the official name of the thing is "The World Series of Poker Presented by Jack Link's Beef Jerky." I had, in effect, been walking around in a big plastic bag ever since I stepped in the Rio. Explained the chronic suffocating feeling.

The company's red and black logo mottled the ESPN studio in the Amazon Room, vivid on the clothing of sponsored players like cattle brands. Jack Link's "Messin' with Sasquatch" commercials were a mainstay of poker TV programming, featuring their mascot Sasquatch as he was humiliated by golfers, campers, and frat boys before putting a Big Foot up their asses. The mascot's meaning? Despite the death of the frontier, and the stifling monotony of modern life, the Savage still walks among us. That, or Betty White was unavailable.

Watch any of ESPN's coverage and you'll encounter "Jack Link's Beef Jerky Wild Card Hand," in which host Norman Chad tries to divine the contents of a hand through betting patterns. The "hole-card cam" was a clutch innovation behind poker's populist boom, allowing viewers to see the players' hands. Before we pierced that veil, televised poker was like watching a baseball game with an invisible ball—i.e., even more boring than watching regular baseball. The hole-card cam allowed for simultaneous commentary—just like real sports! The fans participated in the spectacle, second-guessing, pitting their own calculations against the pros' moves. They learned. They got better. They started playing in the events they watched on TV.

Poker as million-dollar theater, hence the upgrade from Johnny Moss's engraved silver cup to diamond-encrusted bracelets. I was implicated in this big-biz operation. *Grantland*, the magazine that sent me, was owned by ESPN. ESPN was owned by Disney. Which is why they had trouble finding my check. It was floating around the accounting office of Caesars, which was owned by Harrah's, who owned the WSOP. At registration, I'd kept mentioning ESPN and *Grantland* as my benefactors, when the check was cut by Disney. We were all confused.

People asked if I'd be able to keep the money if I cashed at the WSOP. Yes—that had been made clear to me. I wasn't getting paid for the article. My compensation was them paying my entrance fee. Haggle with a lowly freelancer over winnings? Peanuts to the parent corp. I was writing for an entity owned by the company that made millions and millions off WSOP coverage. My words were an advertisement, is one way of looking at it. Raise awareness of the game. Inspire some misfit kid to take up poker. Spread the gospel far and wide. Maybe they'd even hold a circuit game in Anhedonia one day. On the Eastern Coast, a popular vacation spot often free of corpses.

Grantland. ESPN. Disney. It was all in the family.

The House always wins.

It was cool to be at the Rio, to sit in ESPN's studio after watching so much poker on TV, railing at home all those years. I was a fan. That's why I was here. When I returned to the studio on Day 5—

Wait, he's dilly-dallying in the stands on Day 5? Shouldn't he be playing? Spoiler: I didn't win the Main Event. You had suspicions, you say? For one thing, the subtitle of this book would be "The Amazing Life-Affirming Story of an Unremarkable Jerk Who Won the World Series of Poker!" instead of having the word "Death" in it. For another, do these sound like the words of a motherfucker who won a million goddamn dollars?

You'd think I'd include peppier adjectives. If I'd won, you might not be reading this right now. I mean, I would've written this book, artistic imperative and all that, but not so soon. No, I'd still be sailing around the Caribbean on my yacht with some wretched hotties. The Lost Ones, first-round rejects from *Hip Hop Honeys*. Yeah, they look foxy in their drab, ill-fitting overalls, but the talent scouts always take a pass on account of their disquieting smiles and far-off stares. My kind of crowd. We chill on the aft futons, reel in marlin, shake the blender as we mix coladas. The skipper's half in the bag but I don't care, I'll write the book when I get back.

But for those who want to hang on to hope, let's say I was watching Day 5 of an unspecified WSOP, not necessarily 2011 (even though that's when it was).

On Day 5 the TV room, the Amazon, was the last room left. The Main Event had been cut down to 378 players, so they were already packing up. The sad end-game atmosphere of conventions the world over. The 24/7 video display in the rotunda had been wheeled away, the bunting was half ripped down, the gigantic head shots of game legends rolled up until next year. The Pavilion was shut. I peeked in: In the vast, empty hall, union guys stacked the chairs and loaded them onto dollies. No more legions of would-be heroes and their spank-bank visions of poker glory. You were playing the Amazon Room, or you were busto.

Given the number of combatants, the Feature Table was distilled poker prowess. Like Allen Cunningham, five-time bracelet winner, who had stared me down for days from his gigantic head shot on the rotunda wall. Drowsy in person. Unimposing in his white checkered button-down. He was sharing close-ups with Jean-Robert Bellande and Daniel Negreanu, who'd wrangled their poker TV fame into slots on reality shows, *Survivor* and *Millionaire Matchmaker*, respectively. They were more than poker stars, they were TV stars and knew the business of being in front of the camera. Bellande ambled up to the Feature Table, looking slick, trailed by a skinny guy in a black suit: "Is everything all right?" Almost showtime, Mr. Bellande. Bellande asked for a chip count—where's everybody stand before the next level starts?—and posed for a picture with a fan.

The railbirds chirped. Can I get an autograph, Kid Poker? I'd seen Negreanu emanating the last few days, providing wiseacre pull quotes to the press during their blog check-ins, chuckling through an at-table massage, his blond highlights glinting. Relaxed, chipper. He'd been through it all before, this imp. Between hands he and Bellande yukked it up about some Twitter incident, and belittled annoying tournament rules. The Powers That Be were always instituting new protocols, to curb the arms race of who can wear the most sponsored gear on-screen, to regulate table talk. Negreanu was affable, joshing with the table and the fans, but he'd started the day with half the average stack, and was now down to twenty Big Blinds. Then it was fifteen Big Blinds . . .

When the next level started—$6,000/$12,000 blinds, $2,000 antes—I was so programmed that I heard the TV announcer's voice in my head, drowning out the live commentator's. When I watched the broadcast months later, ESPN framed the episode as Kid Poker's Last Stand, with heavy metal guitar to punctuate:

> *Player of the Year! [power chord!] Millions in Tournament winnings! [power chord!] Celebrity and stardom! [Kid Poker holds up wads of cash] Daniel Negreanu has accomplished everything in poker except his biggest and toughest goal—the Main Event! [Kid Poker storms away from a busted hand] Tonight it's put up or shut up for Kid Poker and his dwindling stack. Will he continue to climb poker's highest peak, or will he fall short once again?*

Live, the end of his Main Event was less dramatic. More humble and human-size. The spectator area was just a couple of rows, but the dark cobalt lighting gave them false depth on TV. Friends of the high-performing amateur players at the Feature Table and fans of the big shots jostled for seats. Some of them were on the job.

The Feature Table action was being livestreamed, with a thirty-minute delay. Which meant that anyone watching knew what players had held in this or that showdown a couple of hands back. And they could inform their pals. Sorry to break it to you, but she was bluffing with 5-10 offsuit. What kind of range forced that tall Swede to move All In? Your cronies relay information, texting, waving you over to the rails for a quick huddle, to help navigate course corrections. "Dude, he totally got inside your head thirty-one minutes ago." The hole-card cam strikes again.

Negreanu had no choice but to shove when he got dealt a pair of 10s. Everyone mucked except Rupert Elder, a British pro, who turned over his A7. Elder kept mum, perhaps because he must have been sweltering in that white cable-knit sweater.

Negreanu jumped from his seat, punching the air. "We need a 10 and we're good!" He whirled. "I wanna win this hand really bad! Really bad!" I didn't know if he was addressing his supporters, who loudly rooted from the rails, or the viewers behind the camera feeds, or himself. Maybe he danced for the Poker Gods, as Maud of the Magic River checked the ledgers. Had he been naughty or nice?

The flop was 9-5-3—no help. "This World Series sucks! Every time I'm two to one, I lose!"

Elder said nothing. Negreanu remained the favorite. If there was a Poker God present, it was Tim Old Spice, keeping Elder fresh. The man didn't flinch.

The turn gave Elder a pair of aces. It was no longer two to one.

"He has to catch a 10," the live commentator said, "or he will be eliminated."

"A 10!" Negreanu implored.

The River. It was not a 10. Kid Poker was out.

Bellande shook his head.

"How about a big round of applause for Mr. Daniel Negreanu!" Kid Poker patted Elder on the back with a "Good luck, bro," submitted to a quick exit interview with Kara Scott. Then he was gone.

Which left Cunningham and Bellande as the seniors at the table. Bellande busted the next day in seventy-eighth place. Cunningham busted soon after in sixty-ninth place. They made some money. August rolls around, and it's just another tournament.

Yosemite Sam and his posse had been deposed by young hotshots like Kid Poker, and now Kid Poker had to shake these even younger players off his pants leg. With more than ten million in poker winnings, that was a lot of pants leg, but there were a lot of kids, too. At the Final Table in 2011, the contenders were in their early-to-mid-twenties, except for Badih Bounahra, a forty-nine-year-old amateur who'd squeezed into the lifeboat. The winner was Pius Heinz, a twenty-two-year-old German player who'd started online and was introduced to the game by watching hole-card cams in the Main Event on TV. The last hole-card cam of the 2011 WSOP revealed cards that gave Pius $8 million.

You'll never get a Final Table full of colorful cowboys again. Simple numbers. To make it to the November Nine, the cards need to run too well for you and too poorly for too many other people. Poker dexterity will rescue you from riptides that overwhelmed weak players and driftwood-hugging Robotrons, but you'd still need a surfeit of good fortune.

In a couple of days they'd dismantle the studio, Bubble Wrap the more expensive branding material. Drop it into crates with the rest of the equipment, as if it were a fresh batch of jerky, packed into handy resealable pouches for distribution across the land. Resume the game in November, to celebrate the nine players who endured.

I kept Dexter Choi's business card in my wallet for ten years, until one day I got worried I might lose it. I took it out and never saw it again. On a Thanksgiving '97 trip, I looked for the House of Jerky. It was gone. Pushed out to make room for the Fremont Street Experience, an electronic canopy that covers four blocks of downtown.

At night they turn off the casino marquees and the light show begins, eleven million LEDs blinking out tribute to Vegas history. One light for every bad beat and botched connection this evening, one light for that poker hero cut down, and another for that luckless convention-eer returning to her hotel room alone. Enough lights to spare some for a mad dreamer or two. The Dexter Chois of the world. No one can see what they see, until they build it. If their plans sound ridiculous, if they've over-stepped their abilities and aimed too high, they are not the first in this town to do so.

Tourists foolish enough to be ensnared by the promos for this crummy light show look up for a few minutes, and then it's over. They drift away. The night is young, the city endless, and there are so many more disappointments to savor before dawn.

....

I woke up Tuesday with low M, emotion-wise. I wasn't concerned about my short stack, as I was strangely opti-mistic that I'd get a good run of cards on Day 2B. Now that I'd finished a day of play, I'd come out swinging. But I'd been hit with a powerful case of the local affliction, the symptoms of which consisted of repeatedly mumbling "What the fuck am I doing in Vegas?" until you worked yourself into a desperate froth. I think residents were immune, but tourists were particularly susceptible to this strain of existential Montezuma's revenge.

Coach was up and at 'em on the East Coast. She direct-messaged a pep talk:

Bagged and tagged! Goal! While you are sleeping this morning, I'll research the field. Today's goal: rest and recuperate. Great job.

You've outlasted 2,324 players—3rd largest entry in live history. 1D is largest entry day ever. 4,540 remain—on 2B there will be less.

Chip average looks to be 45K, but don't let this worry you. 23K is nearly an M of 20x pot. You have enough to play and cripple others.

Great 2B table draw! 6 seat with no notable players and no monster stacks. Table low stack 14K. 4 seats shorter than you. Big: 50K. Avg: 25.

Day 2, we'll talk about ways to double up and who to go after. You are in fine shape. You're alive!

We talked on the phone in the afternoon, a debrief on the rest of Day 1. I was still depressed by the Master of Illusion's anticlimactic exit. To play for so long, pay ten grand, wait for the perfect hand, and then have your KK pulverized by a meteor from the deep cold of space: AA.

"You're not going to see that hand again," Coach told me. You saw that maybe once a tournament, and now I'd gotten it out of the way. She gave me homework, Dan Harrington, natch: *Reread DH Vol 1 Pt 5 (betting) p.198-213, 275-286. Vol 2 (zones) 133-155. Get ready to say, 'All in.'*

Call her if I needed anything else. Hit the books (yeah, I'd brought them cross-country with me), get some food, maybe I'd feel better. At 2:34 p.m., Coach sent me a message: "Dan Harrington just busted. Moment of silence, please."

Great.

....

Coach's breakdown of the situation alleviated any remaining stress over my game plan, and I was grateful. Her Southern accent and chipper delivery really sold it. My Vegas melancholy deepened throughout my day off, however. I missed my kid. I was sick of the Rio food. Christ, the All-American Bar and Grille—the flavor profiles of foreign lands had never agreed with me. I wanted to exist one single day on this miserable planet without having the thought, "I should really have the Caesar salad." I should have called my college roommate Shecky—he'd tried to get in on a satellite but no go—to see if he wanted to hang, but I was embroiled in a full-on wallow.

The mere fact of Vegas, its necessity, was an indictment of our normal lives. If we needed this place—to transform into a high roller or a sexy swinger, to be someone else, a winner for once—then certainly the world beyond the desert was a small and mealy place indeed. We shuffled under fluorescent tubes in offices, steered the shopping carts through outlet malls and organic supermarkets while consulting a succession of moronic lists, and wearily collapsed on our beds at night with visions of the Big Score shimmering in our heads. There's a leak in the attic again, the TV's out of warranty, maybe we should get a tutor for Dylan, he's a smart kid but doesn't test well—and then there was Vegas. Vegas will heal us.

I didn't want to be healed, but I knew there was something in the cards I needed. This was the assignment of a lifetime, right? It had never occurred to me that one day I'd play in the World Series of Poker. I was just a home-game scrub. But I loved them, I loved cards. I always had.

Memory is the past with volume control, turn it up, turn it down. Can I make out what I heard in the cards? The martial snap of an expertly shuffled deck, the sleek whisper of laminated paper jetting across the table. Crazy 8s and Spit and then Hearts in college. I was the Bruce Lee of Hearts, no joke, knew all the nerve clusters to paralyze your ass. I'd prowl around the dorm on becalmed afternoons, searching for Hearts players like the disheveled emissary of a ramshackle sect. Our holy text was composed of cut-up newsprint and down-market glossies, but we hit the streets anyway and hoped no one would notice. Everyone was busy studying or calling "their people" back home or whatever, except for me. Cards killed the hours. Then bridge, and then poker, the games that helped me unscramble the secret message: The next card, the next card is the one that will save me.

....

◆

I slept poorly the night of 2A. I had played it safe the first day, stuck to the winners. I hadn't gambled too much. Now I had to reconnect with that old faith, that when the next card turned over, I'd see my future there.

I thought I heard crickets.

. . . .

There was some nice theater to the Ceremonial Unbagging of the Chips at the start of Day 2B. "Dealers, if a player is not present two minutes before start, remove their chips and place the bag on their seat." I was at White 83, Seat 6, and per Coach's assessment, I was still swimming in a tide pool with the guppy luckless and jelly-organism amateurs. No big stacks. Steven Garfinkle had told me that one of the great wonders of poker was that a normal Joe could sit down at a tournament table next to one of their idols. Which was true, it was a beautiful thing, like finding yourself playing [a sport] with [a famous player]. (I stopped following sports once Ty Cobb retired.) But I didn't want to sit next to Jonathan Duhamel.

Country Time was my speed. Country Time, on my right, was a sober, elderly gentleman in a brown sweater, and I did not think he meant me harm. I did a little Alexander to chill me out, breathe in, breathe out, and checked the other stacks through my sunglasses.

Did I neglect to say I was wearing sunglasses? I hadn't the nerve during my trial tourneys, as I felt like a douchebag, but the first time I stepped into the Pavilion I happened to be wearing them, and it felt good. I felt safe. They were nothing special, the ones I'd been wearing for years, but they'd filtered out some of my city's more evil wavelengths many times. The visor in my suit of armor.

Perhaps it is also possible that I have not mentioned the rest of my battle gear. I wore a track jacket. A special track jacket. A few weeks before the Main Event, I set up a solicitation on one of the social media sites:

If you've seen the tournament on ESPN, you know that all the real players wear the names of sponsors on their sweatshirts and caps and T-shirts.

I want to blend in, so I am now accepting sponsors. There are two tiers of sponsorship.

In the Premium "God's Chosen" Sponsorship Level, I will wear your name, enterprise, slogan, or credo on my shirt for $11.25. There are three slots open.

In the Hoi Polloi Sponsorship Level, you can purchase one of 10 Commemorative Signature Bracelets. They will be green or orange in color, I haven't decided which. On the outside, they will bear the slogan KEEP WINNING HANDS. This will "buck you up" when you need it, an imperative, a prayer, or simple statement of fact, depending. On the inner part of the bracelet, where no one can see, they will read STILL SAD INSIDE. This will remind you of the truth.

They will be sold for $4.95 . . .

◆

It has been pointed out that the cost of producing this mer-chandise will exceed the money raised. To which I say, I have never been good at math.

I got a few responses. I didn't get my act together to order the bracelets before I left, but I got the duds. I went to a custom T-shirt joint in Dumbo and handed the designer the specs. I'd have to pay extra for a rush job. She double-checked my chicken-scratch, track jacket first.

"Republic of . . . Ann-hee—"

"Anhedonia," I said.

"What are those?"

"Those are lightning bolts," I said.

She told me to pick out a color for the T-shirt's font, something to accent the brown fabric. I didn't want to clash. Fuck that. She made two suggestions. I picked one.

"That's 'Vegas Gold,'" she said. "Maybe it'll be good luck!"

I wanted diverse sponsors: a person, a business, and a slogan for the back. So I put "WSOP 2011" over the left breast in *Space: 1999* letters, and my pal Nathan Englander's name on the right sleeve—he was in my home game and had been a stalwart ally during Poker Quest. The NYC bookstore McNally Jackson anchored the left sleeve. The bookstore's Twitter feed had offered up a slogan, something like "Crying on National TV Is My Tell," but, uh, the name of the store was shorter so I went with that. The owner had given me some picture books for the kid one time, so it felt right.

Finally, on the back I put "My Other Hand Is Bullets," in an old-timey Western font, which my friend Rob Spillman had suggested. I explained to the designer that "Bullets" was slang for a pair of pocket Aces. I didn't want her to think I was going on a murder spree, or to a panel discussion. I already owned a "This Is More of a Statement Than a Question" T for panel discussions.

When I told Coach about the paraphernalia, she laughed but also suggested that maybe I hold off on wearing the TV shirt until I made it into the money. "It's a bit snarky," she declared. Players were going to target me anyway, because they'd catch on to my inexperience (gee, how?) and because I "didn't look like the average poker player," like a Big Mitch, one hand eternally patting his gut. No point in giving them another reason. Okay, in the money, sure. As it happened, the WSOP cracked down on logos this year, part of the fallout from the Feds' assault on online poker sites. It reduced the sometimes absurd number of patches you saw on the TV shows, which made the grizzled players look like steamer trunks in a '40s movie.

I was going to wear the jacket, though, a snazzy red number with the name of my homeland on the front and the aforementioned lightning bolts, lest anyone doubt where I was coming from.

♦

Finally, I had my talisman. Our last day together, I asked the kid to give me a good-luck charm. I was going to be gone three weeks all told, the longest we'd ever been apart, and I started missing her even before I left. I'd make up the time when I got back, we had years and years ahead of us, but how can you make up moments? I was standing on the terrace outside the convention hall, baking in the merciless Vegas heat and trying to keep a steady signal on my cell, when she told me, "I saw a rainbow, Daddy!" The ex-wife and the kid were in upstate New York, and I knew it had rained because folks were complaining about it on my Twitter feed. Her first rainbow. It hadn't occurred to me that a rainbow was one of the milestones. Unscrewing the training wheels, sure, but light refracted through water vapor? What she felt about it was the important thing. Light refracted through water vapor. Here I was dying in the desert. The kid. What else did I have but the kid?

That last day, I asked her to pick something out from her toys. "I'll keep it on my table and it will give me good luck, and I'll think of you whenever I look at it." She deliberated, and chose a pink flip-flop. It was an inch and a half long, made of soft foam, and dangled from a key chain. It just appeared one day, probably from the bowels of a birthday party goodie bag—there was all sorts of weird little crap in those things, nestled among the

Smarties and renegade Now & Laters. "Can you write something on it?" I asked. "Like 'good luck'?"

She deliberated again, and wrote GO LUCK in a six-year-old's penmanship on the sole of the flip-flop. We let the ink dry.

A pink flip-flop on a key chain. The first day I played, I kept it in my jacket pocket. I couldn't bring myself to put it out there. It was definitely not cowboy, it was the very anti-Brunson made physical. On Day 2B, I pushed the charm up against my $23K. There was invisible stuff tied to the ring besides the pink flip-flop, too, all my psychic baggage on a string, limply rising to the ceiling of the Pavilion like a bouquet of faltering balloons. All right, Luck, I'm waiting.

....

Coach wanted me to double up before dinner to $46K. Despite my prediction that I'd unleash my crazy-psycho betting style in Level 6, the only quirks I added to my play were that new protectiveness toward my blinds (Peck at my blinds, will you, crow? I'll show you!) and a more receptive ear to the siren call of pot odds (It only costs a little more to see the flop . . .).

Yes, Big Mitch, I know it's kid's stuff, but in my cheapo home game you didn't consider these things because the stakes were so low. After the Main Event was over, I played some of the home-game poker that had been my usual fare for so many years. It was bananas. Like if you stuck ten squirrels in a cardboard box, shook it up, and then threw in a deck of acorn-scented Bicycle cards. (You will recall my squirrel antipathy.) Raising 2x the blind—what exactly did you mean by that bet, it was fucking gibberish! Six people seeing the flop? You can't all have Aces. I had become a whining Robotron, trapped with bona fide humans.

At the World Series, of all places, I was finally comprehending the underlying principles I'd been studying, getting the barest glimpse of how they worked, their consequences and power. The deep magic. I had an inkling now of what Coach was saying when she said this place was heaven, what her father meant when he told her Vegas was the center of the universe. I felt it.

Too bad it just ended up costing me chips. Nothing panned out. Someone called me when I had QQ, but other than that I didn't scratch up anything during Level 6. In fact, I lost a bunch. I was down to $14K. I was dying. The blinds were about to shoot up to $300/$600, with a $75 ante. The Wave of Mutilation was gathering force, and I was definitely drowning, not waving, as the poet put it. At the break, I sent a DM: *14.5K . . . Ten M. Okay, coach what do I do?*

I received a short reply: *Call me.*

Out on the terrace with the smokers. You know how

in the literature, once you share blood with a vampire, a psychic link is established whereby he or she can send visions and imperatives? That's cigs, even years later. Anyhoo.

"Hey."

It was the Farting/Burping Guy from Day 1D. He was running bad, $90K down to $50K. "I haven't had a pair of Aces all day," he said. He asked how I was doing.

I told him.

He shrugged and gave a grim smile. "You never know," he said. I'd despised him the day before, touching my stuff, but now we were just two guys in the Main Event, hanging on. He was all right by me.

The 3G limped along. Everybody calling their buddies back home, their spouses, shrinks, giving updates. I couldn't get a signal out. Twitter was dead. Given my low emotional bandwidth, I understood AT&T's difficulties, but hell. Finally a bunch of lazy-ass electrons eked through and I got a stream of DMs:

Shove time. But you have time to wait for a decent hand. I'll run it down for you.

Her next couple of DMs detailed starting combos I should go All In with, pairs, face cards, how to play them in different positions around the table. Under the gun, middle, the button.

You are in all-in shove mode. This is easy. You have one decision and plenty of time to wait for a decent spot.

♦

Doubling up is key, but stealing 2,400 pots with all-in shoves is fine.

New goal: 25K by end of this round. Once you reach this, you can relax and play normal for a little while.

Double up time. One, two, three double-ups and you're a contender. Go get 'em.

I tried to keep it straight. Was that a pair of 7s in early position, or only if there's no raiser? AJ when, whatzit, huh? But Coach believed in me, I was going to do this. If I didn't, I would cease to exist.

At the start of Level 7, I gathered myself. I recalled a steamy Brooklyn summer morning weeks ago, when my physical trainer Kim tried to straighten out the sad, gnarled bone-cloak I called my body. Get into your spine, she said.

Get into your spine.

Get Some Spine.

Patience and Position. I waited. I wasn't the only one with water in his nose. Seat 9 had started out with a stack my size, and he mixed it up in Level 6. Now he was treading water and looking for his shot. He shoved his chips in—and the Wave of Mutilation took him under. Seat 3 was a young dude who'd been staying afloat by attacking blinds, some chips here, some chips there. He went All In, and was sucked down into the bleak fathoms. (You shouldn't wear headphones when swimming, because you can't hear when someone yells, "Shark!") For my part, I got KQ offsuit early in the level . . . and didn't go for it. It didn't feel right, and surely a better hand was rising in the deck, about to bubble up from randomness and bail me out. Right?

It didn't happen. Rags, rags, rags for an hour and a half. Instead of limiting my speech to the word "Raise," now I said, "Can I have some change?" as I slid a $1,000 chip to Seat 5. The Wave of Mutilation washed away my stack, chip by inevitable chip, and I kept calculating and recalculating my M. Was now the time to freak out, shove with anything? Was I being passive, or waiting for my shot? Down to $6K. I wasn't feeling that well. Then I saw them: pocket Aces. Rockets. The selfsame bullets on the T-shirt. I was going to take down this fucking pot.

I went All In . . . and won the blinds and the antes—i.e., bubkes. Bobbed up to $8K, but the swells were about to get much worse.

The announcer informed us there were three more hands until break. The floor managers broke tables on the edges of the White Section; they'd disperse my happy clan soon. I didn't know if it was better to play with these guys or a fresh table. Who knew what kind of behemoth stacks roamed out there in the depths, beyond my little tide pool. I was going to make a move before Level 7 ended, no matter what. As I said, the poker-book advice can be hard to follow—the esoteric slang, the situations you have to experience firsthand in order to appreciate,

♦

the crappy writing. And then there was advice that made perfect sense, like: Before the end of the night, before a break or adjournment for dinner, you can grab a pot because people are distracted and want to split. This made sense to me, more than "suited connectors on the button can be a strong play," because it was sneaky, and I came from a long line of secretive, sneaky bastards. We slinked down the block to steal a cab upstream, left two teaspoons of juice in the carton and put it back in the fridge, and pretended that we didn't use up all the hot water. Sneaky.

I had three chances. It was a Wave of Mutilation: Surf it, motherfucker. My first two cards were no go. White 83 fidgeted as it contemplated the break. Next hand, I think I almost pushed my chips in, but declined. I wasn't feeling it. Players from other tables squeezed out into the hallway. One more chance: K-8, offsuit. Half my table looked at their hands and mucked and departed to have a smoke or take a piss. I pushed—and the new guy in Seat 3, he did nothing at all. He sat. He was the Big Blind this hand, and he was a swiper, green chips in towers.

So the swiper's BB was in the pot. What happens, you may ask, when the swiper becomes the *swipee*? Swiper scrutinized me and asked a question. I didn't catch it, it was some poker nomenclature beyond my ken. I stared into the pot, then past the pot, through the felt, into the void. In general, I had realized, most of my table image was me pretending I was spending a typical afternoon in my crummy, divorced-guy apartment. Just hanging around with a faraway look. Tick tock. Finally he folded. Anticlimactic. It was some chips anyway. Up to $9.6K.

I DM'd Coach on the situation. You may be wondering what Helen was doing in between strategy sessions. She was thousands of miles away in her Upper East Side apartment, gathering intel on the game at her kitchen counter and doing home projects. "I was watching my Twitter feed," she told me later, "and making sure you were not tweeting. Then when the levels started, I would run away. I was so nervous for you! I was listening to books on tape, scouring the floorboards. Cleaning the oven. Doing home projects." She had made what she called her "M-sheet," an index card listing how to bet at different, danger-zone M's, the blind structure at each level. She kept the M-sheet in her pocket for quick consult during my breaks.

Under $8K, she wrote one word: *Worry.*

You're ok, you're ok. But you've got to double up and loosen even more. Here's how:

Once again, she broke down the hands to play, and how.

Do it. Double up. Then double up again, damn it. #toughlove

◆

I blipped out a message through AT&T's "cellular network" and told her I hadn't seen any of those hands, just Aces, so I was due.

Hell yes, you're due. You are not going to bust out of Day 2. You are a shove machine.

You've outlasted 500 players (Matusow, Dunst, Greenstein) for a reason. Patience. I predict 3 double-ups b/f dinner. RUSH dang it!

I want to see you double up and then shove all-in before you've had time to stack your chips. I see it. Rush! Then swordfish.

GOGOGO! I am glued to this computer rooting for you with the blind structure and Ms in my apron pocket.

There you have it. No more negative thinking, despite its centrality in my day-to-day philosophy. I was a player, and I was in this game. I wasn't depressed, I was curating despair. I wasn't half dead, but half alive.

I reentered the Pavilion and waited for the color-up to finish, when they take out all the $25 chips and change them for $100s. Bye-bye chump change. Bye-bye chumps, too.

I started humming that song from *Ocean's Eleven*. I know most classical music from the pop vehicle that introduced me to it, hence "That orgy song from *A Clockwork Orange*" or "That one where Bugs Bunny victimized the opera singer." The aforementioned opera sequence from *The Untouchables*. The tune in question was "Clair de Lune," a tender little number, and I did not mind humming it among the gamblers. If I whistled on the streets in New York, I could hum in the casinos of Las Vegas.

So, Debussy. "Moonshine." It starts off slowly, and you lift with the current, this sort of warm levitating feeling. Then it picks up, cresting to a victorious apex, but it's a curious kind of victory, for even as it approaches fulfillment, each triumphant note is undercut by evanescence, a hint of loss that is contrary to the apparent trajectory of the song, and at the same time its true destination. The eventual collapse of the idea of escape is the real heart of the tune, even as we float joyfully on its evasions. It contained both failure and reward at the same time, and it was okay.

In *Ocean's Eleven*, the movie stars assemble before the Bellagio's dancing waters, the casino's nightly extravaganza of synchronized fountain jets. For the whole flick, the movie stars have been handsome, they have been clever and rude, but now they are quiet. They cannot speak. This was the big one. It was the big job, the heist of a lifetime, and somehow they'd pulled it off. Everything before this was half-assed practice. Everything after will be disappointing postscript. The movie stars stand there looking at the dancing waters, among strangers, the tourists and the squares, the ones who'd never know that a miracle just happened. But these guys knew, they had touched it, even if seconds from now it would change

♦

from *what they did* into *what happened*, become a story they'd rarely share. They'd tell it years from now because they felt safe with their companion, or because they were feeling down and couldn't help themselves. The night is cool, the heart is sliding into nostalgia, and they say, "Did I ever tell you about the time I played in the World Series of Poker?" The awful knowledge that you did what you set out to do, and you would never, ever top it. It was gone the instant you put your hands on it. It was gambling.

The only heist I'd ever pulled was some *Rififi*-type shit to get the kid's tooth from under her pillow and slip some Arby's coupons in there. But I was calm, for a shove machine. This was the round where I'd make my stand. I arranged my chips into a tiny fort. I turned the pink foam flip-flop upside down so I could see what the kid wrote to me.

GO LUCK

(Don't tell me you didn't realize this was a sports movie, the only one I'll ever star in. Maybe you, too, because we're in this together, you and I. But keep in mind it's a '70s sports movie, and you know how those end.)

The blinds were $400/$800 with a $100 ante. I was at 4M, the Wave of Mutilation rising five seats down. The dealer shuffled and . . . I got cards. Two hands into Level 8, I got AK. Big Slick. Now we could begin.

I pretended to think about it, lying like a weatherman, and went All In. Everyone folded except for the swiper. Perhaps he suspected I'd run a game on him that last round before break, made him fold something promising. Here was a duel, unfolding before the table broke, it was a harpoon fight on a disintegrating chunk of ice in the polar seas, I'd seen this on TV. I intended to gut him, and I did. I turned over my AK, he showed his K-whatever, and I bled him on the Flop, and the Turn, and the River. I doubled up to $19K. You bet all your chips, the other guy or gal matches you, and if you win, you get all that plus the blinds and antes: double up. "Swiper, no swiping," as Dora says.

They were about to break the table. The floor manager had our table draws, and he'd distribute them after this next hand. Country Time went All In. He'd done it a few times before, to mucks all around. This time, someone called him. I can't remember what the flop was. All I know is that Country Time was out, and he drifted away.

The dealer was having some trouble sorting through Country Time's stack. Seat 5 said, "I don't know if he's out." Maybe Country Time had chips left.

"He's still there," someone said. Indeed Country Time was, well, taking his time in his departure. There are different types of players. Aggressive. Solid. But there was only one way to walk out of the room when you bust: Absent of dignity, full of shame.

"Should we get him?"

"Count it," the floor manager said.

The dealer moved the chips around.

"Does he have anything left?"

"He's walking slowly."

"We can catch up to him."

We looked over. We looked back at the chips.

"How much does he have?"

"Should we get him?"

No one moved.

"Count it again," the floor manager said.

"He's walking pretty slowly."

Country Time exited the Pavilion. He had a single chip left, $1,000. One of the players asked what was going to happen to it. The floor manager said it would be placed at his seat at his new draw. He'd be swiftly blinded out. It was an unsettling image, the floor guy setting this anonymous chip on the next table and the chip just sitting there, being eroded into smaller chips, and evaporating. Never a face to put to the player formerly known as White 83, Seat 5. You know, Country Time.

The table broke. I liked them now, the gamblers. They were just people. They had intimidated me, but no more. They were better players, dexterous in their manipulation of the underlying principles, they had poker faces they toiled over, but they were just dumb morons like I was, mules walking on their gravel. They put on too much cologne or too little antiperspirant, uploaded stupid photos to Facebook, were riven by doubt and then fortified by an unexpected reversal, wiped ketchup from the corners of their mouths, these messy eaters. They were scared, like I was, of being wiped out, of losing all their chips in hexed confrontation. Mules like me. They carried tokens from home to remind them of what they had left behind, and placed these things next to their chips, and they prayed.

....

I joined Black 6, Seat 4. I didn't say anything and got the same back. This was a real table, they were playing cards here: $100K stacks, whole edifices of $1,000 chips like I'd only seen on the tube. Seat 2 was the table leader, decked out like the Unabomber with his hoodie cinched around his face, mirrored lenses repelling others' eyes. I was the second-shortest stack—the worse-off guy looked queasy. But I'd double up again before dinner, per Coach. I felt giddy, like my skin had become so thin that only the tiniest membrane separated me from the outside, my inner self from the pure poker atmosphere I moved in. I'd pulled one heist, and I'd do it again.

Two hands later, I looked down at a pair of 10s. Okay. Cool. The pot was $2,100. I was in early position. Hands—the ones attached to my wrists, not card hands—please do not tremble or shake. I said, "All In." I was starting to like the sound of that. It was much better than, "Can I get some change?" Everybody folded except for Seat 2, Mr. Sinister, who called in a flash.

Damn. We turned our hands over: He had a pair of 3s. What the hell was that about? But that's how he got to be big stack: He played aggro, and from the glum faces around me, it was paying off.

Neither of us made a set. I won with my 10s, and Mr. Sinister said, "That's been happening to me all day."

Doubled up. I was at $40K, thereabouts, 19M. Out of the danger zone. Level 7 had harrowed me as I waited to shove my chips in. The first half hour of Level 8 had wrung me out, but it was time to get out of what Coach called "small-stack mentality." I no longer had to play like I was trying to escape the space station before it self-destructed, as the chirpy computer voice counted down my M. I knew what it was to be an animal. Time was, when I read about the Donner party or a plane going down in the Andes, I was sickened by tales of survivors eating the dead. Now I knew I'd be all "Pass the hot sauce?" on Day 4. But I was back. I wasn't a fucking animal anymore.

It was an hour and fifteen minutes until dinner. I could do that. Then I got a pair of Aces.

On a rush. Cool. I wasn't going to go All In, I thought, because I could play normal again. I bet $2,200, the table standard for this level. I was going to make some chips.

There were mucks, and then the guy in Seat 7 raised me $8,000. I hadn't seen his face yet. I saw his hands. I saw his chips. He had me matched. Should I go All In? I called his bet, and we saw the flop.

A Queen, an 8, and a 3. No straight, no flush. I was the first to act. He didn't have pocket queens. I don't know how I knew it, but I did. The gift of fear. I bet $10K. He's going to fold, I thought. Instead, he went All In.

I said, "Okay."

"You're All In?" the dealer asked. You had to say it.

"Call."

He had KK. I showed my hand. The table groaned. "I didn't put him on Aces," Mr. Sinister said, with a touch of confusion in his voice.

"I thought maybe he had Ace-Queen," someone else said. They were already consoling Seat 7, down at the other end of the table. "Damn, dude."

The next card was a Jack. For a second I thought, Is he going to get a straight? I was being silly, that was impossible. Three double ups before dinner, just like Coach told me. I had it. He needed two cards to save him, the remaining kings. I was 94 percent favorite to win. But you know how '70s sports movies end.

He got his K.

I was out.

"Aww, man.

"Damn."

"That's a bad beat."

"I didn't think he had Aces," Mr. Sinister repeated, like a fucking idiot. I was starting to think he wasn't a poker maestro, just some guy who'd been getting some good cards, which happened from time to time.

Seat 7 was a portly twenty-something guy with an Australian accent. He came over and shook my hand. "You played that really well," he said. "I didn't think you had Aces."

No, no one knew I had Aces. I could have gone All In before the flop, or after the flop. Then they would have known something was up. Not that he would have folded KK, but still. Betting aside, I think you and I know why they didn't see Aces coming. Why I was unreadable, why they could only guess at my hand.

I have a good poker face because I am half dead inside.

The World Series of Poker's official count of the nations represented at this year's Main Event was ninety-eight. The number had always been off by one. Now the figure was correct. I grabbed my track jacket, jabbed the pink flip-flop in the pocket, and staggered out of the Pavilion. Absent of dignity, full of shame.

....

Like I said, after the heist, all that's left is the disappointing postscript. Normal life. Coach was surprised that I was calling her in the middle of the level. "It's dinner?" I told her the whole thing, what I could remember.

"He Rivered you! On the River!" I reviewed the betting—was there something I should have done differently? "There was no way he was getting away from Kings." Just as I wasn't going to get away from Aces. "There was no way you weren't going to get all your money in that pot." I still think about it, of course. But everybody has hands like that. The failures that stick.

Husband Lex had just gotten home from work. Coach gave the rundown. "I told him it was a good way to go out," she told Lex. As in, better than being washed away by the Wave of Mutilation.

Lex spoke. "Lex just said, 'That's a *terrible* way to go out.'"

I carried out Coach's last order. I finally got to the seafood place and ordered the swordfish. Búzios, it was called. The bartender asked how I was doing. I told him.

"Frankly," I said, "it was pretty exhausting."

"Yeah, these guys come in here, they say, 'I just busted out.' Then they go, 'Thank God, it's over.'"

....

Coach e-mailed me the next day to say she was heading to the Borgata *w/Lex to play the 100k guarantee tourney.* Before I left for Vegas, she'd told me that she was off gambling until September. After her disappointing visit in the early stages of the WSOP, she was taking a break. But being my coach, running scenarios, had put her back in the game. In the fall she pursued the circuit more intensely, even when Lex couldn't make it. That was new. At that December Harrah's event I described earlier, she met Matt. And Matt started coaching Coach.

"When you busted out," she said, "I was horrified. But my first thought was, Good, now I can go to AC!" There's a poker player for you.

I am not Will Smith. Or Michael Clarke Duncan. I cannot heal your limp, and even if I could, I wouldn't. Just because. But I like to think I helped Coach out a little, like she'd helped me. Perhaps Doug Henning had rubbed off on me after all. Magic Doug Henning, who maybe had some Negro blood, I think. Have you seen his hair?

As for me, it was time to go back to Anhedonia. Since busting out, I'd felt my poker knowledge slipping away, "Flowers for Algernon"–style. That too-brief vision of the secret poker world losing resolution, dead pixels blooming. I had been changed, and I did not want to return to who I had been. I needed to hold on to it.

Stay with me, please.

So I did what one does in these situations. In the airport I stopped at Hudson News and bought a souvenir mug, a refrigerator magnet shaped like a flip-flop, and a bottle opener that said "Win Lose or Draw." I'm the sentimental type.

I heard a song, they were playing it in the store, a slow piano tune. There was a TV screen on the wall above the T-shirts, and I saw they were running a loop of the Bellagio dancing water, shot from a helicopter at night, and the music was "Clair de Lune." Courtesy of the Las Vegas Board of Tourism, I imagine.

"Clair" was a cheap date it turned out, the movie now part of the town's mythology. I didn't mind that my private notion had never been mine at all but a popular romance. I couldn't own it. What would Johnny Moss, the first champion of the World Series of Poker, think of how his game had changed over the decades, as it transformed from an intimate competition among buddy-rivals into a multimillion-dollar international event, bigger than any single individual. If Johnny Moss walked into the Pavilion today and saw the thousands of players worrying their stacks, the tables upon tables of hopeful souls, heard the symphony of crickets, I think he'd say, Deal me in. It's not mine, but it's cards.

"Clair de Lune" in a Hudson News franchise was nice exit music from Vegas. It made me feel, how do I put this, good.

There's always next year, right? What the heck, I'll play the circuit, win some tournaments, and come back.

◆

Palm Beach. New Orleans. Tunica. Never heard of Tunica, and maybe that's a good thing. Return to Vegas. Make it to Day 3 this time, make it into the money, it will all work out. Maybe I'll win, and they'll play the national anthem of the Republic of Anhedonia in the Pavilion. I'll stand on the stage in my track jacket, which is now decked out in rhinestones and flapping Vegas Gold fringes, place my hand over my heart (it would take some time to find it), and the speakers in the great hall will broadcast my homeland's song, loud and clear so that everyone can hear it: "NYUH-GUH-UH! UH-GUUHH! NYUH-UGH UGH OH GOD NO NOT AGAIN SSSIIIGGGHHH!"

Try again. It was a very *Bad News Bears* thing to say. Scrappy. Inspiring.

Actually, fuck it.

I learned a lot of things during my long, bizarre trip. About myself and the ways of the world. One, do not hope for change, or the possibility of transcending your everyday existence, because you will fail. Two, if people put their faith in you, you will let them down. And three, everything is a disaster. In short, nothing I hadn't known since childhood, but sometimes you can forget these things when engulfed by a rogue swell of optimism, which happens, if infrequently.

There was a fourth item, but I'll save it for the kid, for when she's older.

ABOUT THE AUTHOR

Colson Whitehead is the author of the novels *The Intuitionist*, *John Henry Days*, *Apex Hides the Hurt*, *Sag Harbor*, and *Zone One*. He has also written a collection of essays called *The Colossus of New York*. His work has appeared in *The New York Times*, *Granta*, *Harper's*, *Grantland*, and *The New Yorker*. A recipient of a Whiting Writers' Award, a MacArthur Fellowship, and a Guggenheim Fellowship, he lives in New York City.